150 Recipes

D0186070

150 BAKING *recipes*
INSPIRED IDEAS FOR EVERYDAY COOKING

150 CAKE *recipes*
INSPIRED IDEAS FOR EVERYDAY COOKING

150 CHICKEN *recipes*
INSPIRED IDEAS FOR EVERYDAY COOKING

150 CUPCAKE & MUFFIN *recipes*
INSPIRED IDEAS FOR EVERYDAY COOKING

150 FAST & SIMPLE *recipes*
INSPIRED IDEAS FOR EVERYDAY COOKING

150 INDIAN *recipes*
INSPIRED IDEAS FOR EVERYDAY COOKING

150 PASTA *recipes*
INSPIRED IDEAS FOR EVERYDAY COOKING

150 SLOW COOKER *recipes*
INSPIRED IDEAS FOR EVERYDAY COOKING

150 STIR-FRY *recipes*
INSPIRED IDEAS FOR EVERYDAY COOKING

150 STUDENT *recipes*
INSPIRED IDEAS FOR EVERYDAY COOKING

150 TAPAS *recipes*
INSPIRED IDEAS FOR EVERYDAY COOKING

150 VEGETARIAN *recipes*
INSPIRED IDEAS FOR EVERYDAY COOKING

CONTENTS

INTRODUCTION

Slow cookers have made a welcome comeback in recent years and their revival looks set to stay, which is good news for all budding cooks. Slow cookers are brilliant for creating marvellous meals with minimum preparation and they are economical to operate, so energy costs are minimal. Less evaporation during cooking in the covered pot means that food stays moist and succulent and there is little chance of it drying out. Slow cookers are versatile too and are readily available in different sizes, shapes and colours, incorporating several (usually three) heat settings/ temperature levels. You can prepare ingredients in the morning, pop them in your slow cooker, then be welcomed home in the evening by the tempting aroma of a perfectly cooked meal!

Slow cooking is suitable for many foods and even the toughest cuts of meat will become meltingly tender, so slow cookers are great for fuss-free cooking on a budget, plus the bonus of cooking a meal in one pot saves on washing up! Slow cooking also retains the goodness of the food, as well as enhancing and developing the flavours.

So, be inspired by our amazing and comprehensive collection of sensational slow cooker recipes, to suit all tastes. Whatever your meal requirements are, be it a starter, main course, dessert or snack, we've got it covered! You'll be astounded at how creative you can be with a slow cooker.

To start things off, whet your appetite with an appealing assortment of poultry dishes, ranging from classic dishes such as Chicken Noodle Soup and Slow Roast Chicken, to some more elaborate eats like Duckling with Apples.

Next up is a selection of magnificent meat dishes, ideal for families or sharing with friends, including soups, stews, goulashes, ribs, roulades and burritos. Be tempted by superb staples including Boston Baked Beans, Ham Cooked in Cider and Beef in Beer, or go global and enjoy ever-popular Spicy Pulled Pork or Thai Beef Curry.

A chapter encompassing an assortment of fabulous fish and seafood dishes features flavour-packed Salmon Chowder and Jambalaya, or opt for more exotic creations like Red Snapper with Fennel and Moroccan Sea Bream.

For those who prefer meat-free meals, our selection of vibrant and tasty meatless recipes is sure to be popular. Featuring a creative choice of soups, spreads, medleys, casseroles, curries and bakes, take your pick from tempting dishes like Italian Bread Soup, Wild Mushroom Lasagne and Pumpkin Risotto.

Finally, tantalize your tastebuds with our scrumptious selection of delicious desserts, popular puddings and must-have bakes. Indulge in delights such as Blushing Pears, Carrot Cake and Strawberry Cheesecake, or enjoy devouring Double Chocolate Cookies and sumptuous Chocolate Fondue.

Helpful Hints

Always read the manufacturer's instructions before you begin, as each slow cooker model will vary slightly. The guidelines will include important advice on preheating your slow cooker as each necessary, as well as providing information on which heat setting to use. You can pick up handy hints and tips for care and maintenance too.

The size and capacity of slow cookers varies, so allowances should be made for the differences in size and internal volume of the model you are using. You may need to adjust the cooking times slightly or the volume of liquid used in recipes, so read the manufacturer's instructions for more specific advice on your model.

With poultry dishes, always make sure the poultry is thoroughly cooked and tender before serving. Ensure the juices run clear and are piping hot and that there are no signs of pinkness when a skewer or fork is inserted into the thickest part of the meat. If the juices are pink or there are traces of blood, continue cooking until the juices run clear.

POULTRY DISHES

CHICKEN NOODLE SOUP

Serves: 4 **Prep: 25 mins** **Cook: 5 hours 35 mins**

Ingredients

1 onion, diced

2 celery sticks, diced

2 carrots, diced

1 kg/2 lb 4 oz oven-ready chicken

700 ml/1¼ pints hot chicken stock

115 g/4 oz dried egg tagliatelle

salt and pepper

2 tbsp chopped fresh dill, plus extra to garnish

Method

1 Place the onion, celery and carrots in the slow cooker. Season the chicken all over with salt and pepper and place on top. Pour the stock over. Cover and cook on low for 5 hours.

2 Leaving the juices in the slow cooker, carefully lift out the chicken and remove the meat from the carcass, discarding the bones and skin. Cut the meat into bite-sized pieces.

3 Skim the excess fat from the juices, then return the chicken to the slow cooker. Turn the setting to high.

4 Bring a large saucepan of lightly salted water to the boil. Add the pasta, bring back to the boil and cook for 8–10 minutes, or until tender but still firm to the bite. Drain, add to the slow cooker and stir well.

5 Add the dill to the soup and stir well. Cover and cook on high for a further 20 minutes. Garnish with extra dill and serve immediately.

★ **Variation**

This recipe can be adapted to use whatever vegetables are in season. You can also vary the type of pasta used, if wished, for an equally delicious winter warmer.

POULTRY DISHES

CHICKEN TORTILLA SOUP

Serves: 4-6   **Prep: 20 mins**   **Cook: 4¼–8¼ hours**

Ingredients

1 tbsp vegetable oil

1 onion, diced

1 tsp chilli powder

1 tsp salt

½ tsp ground cumin

2 tbsp tomato purée

850 ml/1½ pints chicken stock

400 g/14 oz canned chopped tomatoes

1 green chilli, cored, deseeded and finely chopped

450 g/1 lb bone-in, skinless chicken thighs

40 g/1½ oz tortilla chips, broken into small pieces, plus extra to serve

To serve

1 ripe avocado, diced

chopped fresh coriander

1 lime, cut into wedges

Method

1 Heat the oil in a large frying pan over a medium–high heat. Add the onion and cook, stirring occasionally, for about 5 minutes, until soft. Add the chilli powder, salt, cumin and tomato purée and cook, stirring, for a further 1 minute. Add one third of the stock to the pan and bring to the boil, stirring and scraping up any brown bits from the base of the pan.

2 Transfer the mixture to the slow cooker. Add the remaining stock, the tomatoes, chilli, chicken and tortilla chips, then cover and cook on high for about 4 hours or on low for about 8 hours, until the chicken is cooked through and very tender.

3 Lift out the chicken using a slotted spoon, remove and discard the bones and shred the meat. Return the chicken to the slow cooker, cover and heat on high for about 5 minutes, until heated through. Serve immediately, accompanied by diced avocado, chopped coriander, lime wedges and tortilla chips.

SPICY CHICKEN & CHEESE DIP

Serves: 6–8   **Prep: 15 mins**   **Cook: 2 hours 20 mins**

Ingredients

450 g/1 lb Gouda cheese, coarsely grated

225 g/8 oz cooked chicken breast, diced

225 ml/8 fl oz chunky salsa, hot or mild to taste

225 ml/8 fl oz soured cream

3 spring onions, thinly sliced, to garnish

chopped fresh coriander, to garnish

tortilla chips, to serve

Method

1 Put the cheese, chicken and salsa into the slow cooker, stir to mix well, cover and cook on low for 2 hours.

2 Stir in the soured cream, re-cover and cook on high for a further 20 minutes, until heated through.

3 Serve hot, garnished with the spring onions and coriander, with tortilla chips for dipping.

CHILLI PEPPERS STUFFED WITH TURKEY

Serves: 4

Prep: 25 mins, plus standing

Cook: 2 hours 20 mins

Ingredients

4 large poblano or pasilla chillies

1 tbsp vegetable oil

1 onion, diced

450 g/1 lb fresh turkey mince

1 tsp ground cumin

1 tsp mild chilli powder

1 tsp crumbled dried oregano

1 tsp salt

225 ml/8 fl oz salsa, hot or mild to taste

115 g/4 oz mature Cheddar cheese, grated

4 large eggs, lightly beaten

2 tbsp plain flour

175 ml/6 fl oz canned evaporated milk

Method

1 Preheat the grill to high. Put the chillies on a baking sheet, place under the preheated grill and cook for 3–5 minutes on each side, until the skin begins to blister and blacken. Remove from the grill, place in a bowl, and cover with clingfilm. Leave to steam for about 10 minutes, until cool enough to handle, then peel off the skins. Make a slit down one side of each chilli to open it up and remove the stem and seeds.

2 Heat the oil in a large frying pan over a medium–high heat. Add the onion and cook, stirring, for about 5 minutes, until soft. Add the turkey and cook, breaking up the meat with a wooden spoon, for about 4 minutes, or until brown. Stir in the cumin, chilli powder, oregano and salt and cook for a further 1 minute. Stir in the salsa and three quarters of the cheese.

3 Lay the chillies cut side up on a work surface and stuff each one equally with the turkey mixture. Place the chillies in the slow cooker in a single layer.

4 Put the eggs, flour and evaporated milk into a mixing bowl and whisk together. Pour the egg mixture over the chillies and top with the remaining cheese. Cover and cook on low for 2 hours, until puffed and golden brown.

SWEET & SOUR CHICKEN WINGS

Serves: 4–6   **Prep: 20 mins**   **Cook: 5 hours 10 mins**

Ingredients

1 kg/2 lb 4 oz chicken wings, tips removed

2 celery sticks, chopped

700 ml/1¼ pints hot chicken stock

2 tbsp cornflour

3 tbsp white wine vinegar or rice vinegar

3 tbsp dark soy sauce

5 tbsp sweet chilli sauce

55 g/2 oz soft light brown sugar

400 g/14 oz canned pineapple chunks in juice, drained

200 g/7 oz canned sliced bamboo shoots, drained and rinsed

½ green pepper, deseeded and thinly sliced

½ red pepper, deseeded and thinly sliced

salt

steamed pak choi, to serve

Method

1 Put the chicken wings and celery in the slow cooker and season to taste with salt. Pour in the stock, cover and cook on low for 5 hours.

2 Drain the chicken wings, reserving 350 ml/12 fl oz of the stock, and keep warm. Pour the reserved stock into a saucepan and stir in the cornflour. Add the vinegar, soy sauce and chilli sauce. Place over a medium heat and stir in the sugar. Cook, stirring constantly, for 5 minutes, or until the sugar has dissolved completely and the sauce is thickened, smooth and clear.

3 Reduce the heat, stir in the pineapple, bamboo shoots and peppers and simmer gently for 2–3 minutes. Add the chicken wings and mix until they are thoroughly coated, then transfer to warmed serving bowls. Serve immediately with pak choi.

BARBECUE CHICKEN

Serves: 4–6   **Prep: 15 mins**   **Cook: 3 hours**

Ingredients

8 skinless chicken
drumsticks or thighs

3 tbsp tomato purée

2 tbsp clear honey

1 tbsp Worcestershire sauce

juice of ½ lemon

½ tsp crushed dried chillies

1 garlic clove, crushed

salt and pepper

Method

1 Using a sharp knife, cut slashes into the thickest parts of the chicken flesh.

2 Mix the tomato purée, honey, Worcestershire sauce, lemon juice, chillies and garlic together and season to taste with salt and pepper. Add the chicken and toss well to coat evenly.

3 Arrange the chicken in the slow cooker, cover and cook on high for 3 hours.

4 Remove the chicken with a slotted spoon and place in a warmed bowl. Skim any fat from the juices in the slow cooker, and then spoon the juices over the chicken. Serve immediately.

POULTRY DISHES

CHICKEN QUESADILLAS

Serves: 4

Prep: 25 mins, plus marinating

Cook: 2 hours 10 mins

Ingredients

4 skinless, boneless chicken breasts

½ tsp crushed dried chillies

2 garlic cloves, crushed

2 tbsp chopped fresh parsley

2 tbsp olive oil

350 g/12 oz cherry tomatoes

4 large wheat tortillas

250 g/9 oz mozzarella cheese

salt and pepper

Method

1 Place the chicken in a bowl with the chillies, garlic, parsley and 1 tablespoon of the olive oil, and turn to coat evenly. Cover and leave in the refrigerator to marinate for at least 1 hour, or overnight.

2 Tip the tomatoes into the slow cooker and arrange the chicken breasts on top. Season to taste with salt and pepper. Cover and cook on high for 2 hours, or until tender.

3 Remove the chicken and shred the meat using two forks. Place on one side of each tortilla and top with the tomatoes. Chop or tear the mozzarella and arrange on top. Moisten the edges of the tortillas and fold over to enclose the filling.

4 Brush a griddle or large frying pan with the remaining oil and place over a medium heat. Add the quesadillas to the pan and cook until golden, turning once. Cut into wedges and serve immediately with any remaining juices spooned over.

POULTRY DISHES

CHICKEN PARMIGIANA

Serves: 4   **Prep: 15 mins**   **Cook: 8¼–9¼ hours**

Ingredients

4 chicken portions, about 250 g/9 oz each

100 ml/3½ fl oz olive oil

3 red onions, thinly sliced

2 garlic cloves, finely chopped

1 red pepper, deseeded and thinly sliced

115 g/4 oz mushrooms, sliced

2 tsp chopped fresh thyme

1 tbsp chopped fresh flat-leaf parsley

400 g/14 oz canned chopped tomatoes

4 tbsp dry white vermouth

425 ml/15 fl oz chicken stock

85 g/3 oz Parmesan cheese, grated

salt and pepper

cooked pappardelle, to serve

Method

1 Season the chicken with salt and pepper to taste. Heat the oil in a large heavy-based saucepan. Add the chicken and cook over a medium heat for 5–6 minutes on each side, until evenly browned. Using tongs, transfer the chicken to the slow cooker.

2 Add the onions, garlic, red pepper, mushrooms, thyme, parsley, tomatoes, vermouth and stock to the pan. Season to taste with salt and pepper and bring to the boil, stirring occasionally. Transfer the mixture to the slow cooker, cover and cook on low for 8–9 hours, until the chicken is cooked through and tender.

3 Transfer to warmed plates and sprinkle over the Parmesan. Serve immediately with pappardelle.

CHICKEN IN WHITE WINE

Serves: 4–6 | **Prep: 20 mins** | **Cook: 5 hours 35 mins–6 hours 35 mins**

Ingredients

2 tbsp plain flour

1 chicken, weighing 1.6 kg/3 lb 8 oz, cut into 8 pieces

55 g/2 oz unsalted butter

1 tbsp sunflower oil

4 shallots, finely chopped

12 button mushrooms, sliced

2 tbsp brandy

500 ml/18 fl oz Riesling wine

250 ml/9 fl oz double cream

salt and pepper

cooked green vegetables, to serve

Method

1 Put the flour into a polythene bag and season to taste. Add the chicken, in batches, and shake well to coat. Transfer to a plate.

2 Heat half the butter with the oil in a heavy-based frying pan. Add the chicken and cook over a medium–high heat, turning frequently, for 10 minutes, until golden. Transfer to a plate.

3 Wipe out the pan with kitchen paper, then return to the heat and melt the remaining butter. Add the shallots and mushrooms and cook, stirring, for 3 minutes. Return the chicken to the pan and remove it from the heat. Warm the brandy in a small ladle, ignite and pour it over the chicken, shaking the pan gently until the flames have died down.

4 Return the pan to the heat and pour in the wine. Bring to the boil over a low heat, scraping up any sediment from the base of the pan. Transfer to the slow cooker, cover and cook on low for 5–6 hours, until the chicken is cooked through. Transfer to a dish and keep warm.

5 Skim off any fat from the surface of the cooking liquid and pour into a saucepan. Stir in the cream and bring just to the boil over a low heat and pour over the chicken. Serve with green vegetables.

POULTRY DISHES

TURKEY BREAST WITH BACON, LEEKS & PRUNES

Serves: 6–8　　　　**Prep: 25 mins**　　　　**Cook: 5 hours 20 mins–9 hours 20 mins, plus resting**

Ingredients

115 g/4 oz bacon rashers

2 leeks, trimmed, white and light green parts, thinly sliced

1 skinless, bone-in turkey breast (about 1.8 kg/4 lb)

30 g/1 oz plain flour

1 tbsp olive oil, if needed

12 stoned prunes, halved (quartered, if large)

1 tsp crumbled dried thyme or 1 tbsp finely chopped fresh thyme

225 ml/8 fl oz chicken stock

salt and pepper

Method

1 Heat a frying pan over a medium–high heat, then add the bacon and cook until just crisp. Remove from the pan, drain on kitchen paper, then chop or crumble into small pieces.

2 Add the leeks to the pan and cook in the bacon fat over a medium–high heat, stirring frequently, for about 5 minutes, or until soft.

3 Season the turkey well with salt and pepper and dredge with the flour. If needed, add the oil to the pan, then add the turkey and cook on one side for 4–5 minutes, until brown. Turn and cook on the other side for a further 4–5 minutes, until brown.

4 Place the turkey in the slow cooker together with the leeks, bacon, prunes and thyme. Add the stock, cover and cook on high for about 5 hours or on low for about 9 hours.

5 Remove the turkey from the slow cooker and leave to rest for 5 minutes. Slice and serve with some of the sauce, including the prunes and bits of bacon, spooned over the top.

CHIPOTLE CHICKEN STEW

Serves: 4-6　　　　**Prep: 25 mins,**　　　　**Cook: 4¼ hours**
　　　　　　　　　　　plus soaking

Ingredients

200 g/7 oz dried haricot
beans, soaked overnight

1 large onion, sliced

1 dried chipotle pepper,
soaked for 20 minutes,
then drained and finely
chopped

1.5 kg/3 lb 5 oz oven-ready
chicken

200 ml/7 fl oz hot chicken
stock

400 g/14 oz canned
chopped tomatoes

1 tsp ground cumin

salt and pepper

Method

1 Drain and rinse the beans and place in a
saucepan, cover with cold water and bring to
the boil. Boil rapidly for 10 minutes, then remove
from the heat and drain and rinse again.

2 Transfer the beans to the slow cooker and
add the onion and chipotle pepper. Place
the chicken on top, pour over the stock and
tomatoes with their can juices, sprinkle with
cumin and season to taste with salt and pepper.

3 Cover and cook on high for 4 hours. Carefully
remove the chicken and cut into eight pieces.
Skim the excess fat from the juices and taste and
adjust the seasoning, if necessary.

4 Spoon the beans into a warmed serving dish,
top with the chicken and spoon the juices over.
Serve immediately.

CHICKEN BREASTS STUFFED WITH HERBED GOAT'S CHEESE

Serves: 4 **Prep: 25 mins** **Cook: 2 hours 10 mins–4 hours 10 mins**

Ingredients

225 g/8 oz soft, fresh goat's cheese

10 g/¼ oz fresh basil leaves, finely chopped

2 spring onions, thinly sliced

2 garlic cloves, finely chopped

4 boneless, skinless chicken breasts

2 tbsp olive oil

200 g/7 oz chard, central ribs removed, cut into wide ribbons

225 ml/8 fl oz dry white wine, chicken stock or water

salt and pepper

Method

1 Put the cheese, basil, spring onions and garlic into a mixing bowl and stir to combine.

2 Lay the chicken breasts flat on a chopping board. Working with one breast at a time, place your hand on top of the breast and press down to keep it in place. With the other hand, using a large, sharp knife, slice the breast horizontally, leaving one edge intact like a hinge.

3 Open the butterflied breasts and spoon equal amounts of the cheese mixture onto one half of each. Fold closed and secure with wooden cocktail sticks or kitchen string. Season to taste with salt and pepper.

4 Heat the oil in a large frying pan over a medium–high heat until very hot, then add the chicken. Cook on one side for 4 minutes, until brown, then turn and cook on the other side for a further 4 minutes, until brown.

5 Put the chard and the wine into the slow cooker. Arrange the stuffed chicken breasts on top of the chard, cover and cook on high for about 2 hours or on low for about 4 hours, until the chicken is cooked through. Serve immediately.

POULTRY DISHES

CHICKEN BONNE FEMME

Serves: 6   **Prep: 25 mins**   **Cook: 5 hours 35 mins–
6 hours 35 mins**

Ingredients

1 chicken, weighing
1.8 kg/4 lb

55 g/2 oz butter

2 tbsp olive oil

650 g/1 lb 7 oz small white
onions, peeled

650 g/1 lb 7 oz small new
potatoes

175 g/6 oz bacon, diced

500 ml/18 fl oz dry
white wine

1 bouquet garni

500 ml/18 fl oz hot chicken
stock

salt and pepper

chopped fresh flat-leaf
parsley, to garnish

Method

1 Season the chicken inside and out with salt and
pepper. Melt half the butter with the oil in a large
frying pan. Add the chicken and cook over a
medium heat, turning frequently, for 8–10 minutes,
until evenly browned. Remove from the pan and
put it into the slow cooker, breast-side down.

2 Add the onions, potatoes and bacon to the
pan and cook, stirring frequently, for 10 minutes,
until lightly browned. Pour in the wine, season to
taste with salt and pepper and add the bouquet
garni. Bring to the boil, then transfer the mixture
to the slow cooker. Pour in the hot stock. Cover
and cook on high, turning the chicken once
halfway through cooking, for 5–6 hours, until the
chicken is tender and cooked through.

3 Using a slotted spoon, transfer the vegetables
and bacon to a warmed bowl. Carefully remove
the chicken and put it on a warmed serving dish.
Remove and discard the bouquet garni.

4 Measure 600 ml/1 pint of the cooking liquid, pour
it into a saucepan and bring to the boil. Boil until
slightly reduced, then whisk in the remaining
butter, a little at a time. Pour the sauce into a
sauceboat. Carve the chicken and serve with
the bacon and vegetables. Garnish with parsley
and serve immediately with the sauce.

POULTRY DISHES

CHICKEN & DUMPLINGS

Serves: 4   **Prep: 25 mins**   **Cook: 4¾ hours**

Ingredients

2 tbsp olive oil

1 large onion, thinly sliced

2 carrots, cut into
2-cm/¾-inch chunks

225 g/8 oz French beans,
cut into 2.5-cm/1-inch
lengths

4 skinless, boneless chicken
breasts

300 ml/10 fl oz hot chicken
stock

salt and pepper

Dumplings

200 g/7 oz self-raising flour

100 g/3½ oz shredded suet

4 tbsp chopped
fresh parsley

Method

1 Heat 1 tablespoon of oil in a frying pan, add the onion and fry over a high heat for 3–4 minutes, or until golden. Place in the slow cooker with the carrots and beans.

2 Add the remaining oil to the pan, then add the chicken breasts and fry until golden, turning once. Arrange on top of the vegetables in a single layer, season well with salt and pepper and pour over the stock. Cover and cook on low for 4 hours.

3 Turn the slow cooker up to high while making the dumplings. Sift the flour into a bowl and stir in the suet and parsley. Season to taste with salt and pepper. Stir in just enough cold water to make a fairly firm dough, mixing lightly. Divide into 12 and shape into small balls.

4 Arrange the dumplings on top of the chicken, cover and cook for 30 minutes on high. Serve immediately.

POULTRY DISHES

TURKEY HASH

Serves: 4   **Prep: 15 mins**   **Cook: 7 hours 5 mins**

Ingredients

1 tbsp olive oil

500 g/1 lb 2 oz turkey mince

1 large red onion, diced

550 g/1 lb 4 oz butternut squash, diced

2 celery sticks, sliced

500 g/1 lb 2 oz potatoes, peeled and diced

3 tbsp Worcestershire sauce

2 bay leaves

salt and pepper

Method

1 Heat the oil in a frying pan, add the turkey and fry over a high heat, stirring, until broken up and lightly browned all over.

2 Place all the vegetables in the slow cooker then add the turkey and pan juices. Add the Worcestershire sauce and bay leaves and season to taste with salt and pepper. Cover and cook on low for 7 hours. Serve immediately.

CHICKEN & APPLE POT

Serves: 4 **Prep: 25 mins** **Cook: 7 hours 40 mins**

Ingredients

1 tbsp olive oil

4 chicken portions, about 175 g/6 oz each

1 onion, chopped

2 celery sticks, roughly chopped

1½ tbsp plain flour

300 ml/10 fl oz clear apple juice

150 ml/5 fl oz chicken stock

1 cooking apple, cored and cut into quarters

2 bay leaves

1–2 tsp clear honey

1 yellow pepper, deseeded and cut into chunks

salt and pepper

To garnish

1 large or 2 medium eating apples, cored and sliced

1 tbsp melted butter

2 tbsp demerara sugar

1 tbsp chopped fresh mint

Method

1 Heat the oil in a heavy-based frying pan. Add the chicken and cook over a medium–high heat, turning frequently, for 10 minutes, until golden brown. Transfer to the slow cooker. Add the onion and celery to the pan and cook over a low heat for 5 minutes, until softened. Sprinkle in the flour and cook for 2 minutes, then remove the pan from the heat.

2 Gradually stir in the apple juice and stock, then return the pan to the heat and bring to the boil. Stir in the cooking apple, bay leaves and honey and season to taste. Pour the mixture over the chicken in the slow cooker, cover and cook on low for 6½ hours, until the chicken is tender and cooked through. Stir in the pepper, re-cover and cook on high for 45 minutes.

3 Shortly before serving, preheat the grill. Brush one side of the eating apple slices with half the melted butter and sprinkle with half the sugar. Cook under the preheated grill for 2–3 minutes, until the sugar has caramelized. Turn the slices over with tongs, brush with the remaining butter and sprinkle with the remaining sugar. Grill for a further 2 minutes. Transfer the stew to warmed plates and garnish with the caramelized apple slices and the mint. Serve immediately.

CHICKEN & MUSHROOM STEW

Serves: 4   **Prep: 20 mins**   **Cook: 7 hours 35 mins**

Ingredients

15 g/½ oz unsalted butter

2 tbsp olive oil

1.8 kg/4 lb skinless chicken portions

2 red onions, sliced

2 garlic cloves, finely chopped

400 g/14 oz canned chopped tomatoes

2 tbsp chopped fresh flat-leaf parsley

6 fresh basil leaves, torn

1 tbsp sun-dried tomato purée

150 ml/5 fl oz red wine

225 g/8 oz mushrooms, sliced

salt and pepper

Method

1 Heat the butter and oil in a heavy-based frying pan. Add the chicken, in batches if necessary, and cook over a medium–high heat, turning frequently, for 10 minutes, until golden brown all over. Using a slotted spoon, transfer the chicken to the slow cooker.

2 Add the onions and garlic to the frying pan and cook over a low heat, stirring occasionally, for 10 minutes, until golden. Add the tomatoes with their can juices, stir in the parsley, basil, tomato purée and wine and season to taste with salt and pepper. Bring to the boil, then pour the mixture over the chicken.

3 Cover the slow cooker and cook on low for 6½ hours. Stir in the mushrooms, re-cover and cook on high for 30 minutes, until the chicken is tender and the vegetables are cooked through. Taste and adjust the seasoning if necessary and serve immediately.

CHICKEN WITH OLIVES & SUN-DRIED TOMATOES

Serves: 4   **Prep: 25 mins**   **Cook: 4½–8½ hours**

Ingredients

900 g/2 lb skinless, bone-in chicken thighs or drumsticks, or a combination

1 tsp salt

½ tsp pepper

30 g/1 oz plain flour

2 tbsp olive oil, plus extra if needed

1 onion, diced

3 garlic cloves, finely chopped

125 ml/4 fl oz dry white wine

800 g/1 lb 12 oz canned chopped tomatoes

115 g/4 oz stoned Kalamata olives, quartered

75 g/2¾ oz sun-dried tomatoes, chopped

fresh basil leaves, to garnish

cooked pasta, to serve

Method

1 Season the chicken with half the salt and the pepper. Place the flour in a polythene bag, add the chicken pieces, in batches, if necessary, then hold the top securely closed and shake well to coat.

2 Heat the oil in a large frying pan over a medium–high heat. Add the chicken pieces and cook on one side for about 4 minutes, until brown. Turn and cook on the other side for about 4 minutes, until brown. Place the chicken in the slow cooker.

3 Add some more oil to the pan if needed, then add the onion and garlic and sauté over a medium heat for 15 minutes, until soft. Add the wine and bring to the boil. Cook, stirring and scraping up any sediment from the base of the pan, for about 2 minutes. Add the canned tomatoes, olives, sun-dried tomatoes and the remaining salt and cook, stirring, for about 1 minute.

4 Add the mixture to the slow cooker on top of the chicken. Cover and cook on high for 4 hours or on low for 8 hours. Serve immediately with pasta, garnished with basil.

TURKEY CHILLI WITH SWEET POTATOES

Serves: 4–6   **Prep: 20 mins**   **Cook: 4 hours 10 mins– 8 hours 10 mins**

Ingredients

1 tbsp vegetable oil

1 onion, diced

675 g/1 lb 8 oz turkey mince

70 g/2½ oz tomato purée

1 tbsp mild chilli powder

1 tsp ground cumin

2 canned chipotle chillies in adobo sauce, deseeded and diced, plus 2 teaspoons of the adobo sauce (or substitute 1 tsp ground chipotles)

1 tsp salt

400 g/14 oz canned chopped tomatoes

450 ml/16 fl oz chicken stock

1 large sweet potato (about 225 g/8 oz), diced

To serve

fresh coriander

soured cream

grated Cheddar cheese

diced avocado

finely chopped red onion

Method

1 Heat the oil in a large frying pan. Add the onion and cook, stirring, for about 5 minutes, until soft. Add the turkey and cook, breaking up the meat with a wooden spoon, for about 4 minutes, until brown. Stir in the tomato purée, chilli powder, cumin, chillies and adobo sauce, and salt and cook for a further 1 minute.

2 Transfer the mixture to the slow cooker. Stir in the tomatoes, stock and sweet potato. Cover and cook on high for 4 hours or on low for 8 hours. Serve immediately, accompanied by the coriander, soured cream, cheese, avocado and red onion.

CHICKEN WITH RED PEPPER & BROAD BEANS

Serves: 4　　　　**Prep: 25 mins**　　　　**Cook: 7 hours 40 mins–7 hours 55 mins**

Ingredients

1½ tbsp plain flour

4 chicken portions, about 175 g/6 oz each

2 tbsp olive oil

1 onion, chopped

2–3 garlic cloves, chopped

1 fresh red chilli, deseeded and chopped

225 g/8 oz chorizo or other spicy sausages, skinned and cut into small chunks

300 ml/10 fl oz chicken stock

150 ml/5 fl oz dry white wine

1 tbsp dark soy sauce

1 large red pepper, deseeded and sliced into rings

225 g/8 oz shelled broad beans

25 g/1 oz rocket or baby spinach leaves

salt and pepper

Method

1 Spread out the flour on a plate and season well with salt and pepper. Toss the chicken thoroughly in the flour, shaking off any excess. Reserve any remaining flour.

2 Heat half the oil in a heavy-based frying pan, add the chicken portions and cook over a medium–high heat, turning frequently, for 10 minutes, or until golden brown. Add a little more oil during cooking if necessary. Transfer the chicken to the slow cooker.

3 Add the remaining oil to the frying pan. Add the onion, garlic and chilli and cook over a low heat, stirring occasionally, for 5 minutes, until softened. Add the chorizo and cook, stirring frequently, for a further 2 minutes. Sprinkle in the remaining flour and cook, stirring constantly, for 2 minutes, then remove from the heat. Gradually stir in the stock, wine and soy sauce, then return the pan to the heat and bring to the boil, stirring constantly. Pour the onion mixture over the chicken, then cover and cook on low for 6½ hours.

4 Add the red pepper and beans to the slow cooker, re-cover and cook on high for 45–60 minutes, until the chicken and vegetables are cooked through. Season to taste with salt and pepper. Stir in the rocket and serve.

POULTRY DISHES

CHICKEN PAPRIKA

Serves: 4   **Prep: 25 mins**   **Cook: 6 hours 20 mins–9 hours 20 mins**

Ingredients

900 g/2 lb skinless, bone-in chicken thighs or drumsticks, or a combination

1 tsp salt

½ tsp pepper

70 g/2½ oz plain flour

2 tbsp vegetable oil

1 tbsp butter

1 large onion, diced

3 tbsp paprika

2 tbsp tomato purée

225 ml/8 fl oz chicken stock

125 ml/4 fl oz soured cream

finely chopped fresh dill, to garnish

cooked egg noodles or dumplings, to serve

Method

1 Season the chicken with ½ teaspoon of salt and ½ teaspoon of pepper. Place the flour in a polythene bag, add the chicken pieces, in batches, if necessary, then hold the top securely closed and shake well to coat.

2 Heat the oil in a large frying pan over a medium–high heat. Add the chicken pieces and cook on one side for about 4 minutes, until brown. Turn and cook on the other side for about 4 minutes, until brown. Place the chicken in the slow cooker.

3 Add the butter to the pan and heat over a medium–high heat, until melted. Add the onion and cook, stirring occasionally, for about 5 minutes, until soft. Add the paprika, tomato purée and the remaining salt, and cook, stirring, for about 1 minute.

4 Add the stock and bring to the boil, stirring and scraping up the sediment from the base of the pan. Cook for about 1 minute, then pour the onion mixture into the slow cooker over the chicken pieces. Cover and cook on high for 6 hours or on low for 9 hours.

5 Just before serving, stir in the soured cream. Garnish with dill and serve immediately with noodles.

POULTRY DISHES

TURKEY MEATLOAF

Serves: 4   **Prep: 20 mins**   **Cook: 4 hours**

Ingredients

oil, for greasing
600 g/1 lb 5 oz turkey mince
1 onion, finely chopped
55 g/2 oz porridge oats
2 tbsp chopped fresh sage
2 tbsp Worcestershire sauce
1 egg, beaten
salt and pepper

Method

1 Grease and line a 900-g/2-lb loaf tin, or a tin that fits into your slow cooker.

2 Mix the remaining ingredients together and season to taste with salt and pepper.

3 Spoon the mixture into the tin and smooth the top level with a palette knife.

4 Place the loaf in the slow cooker and place a piece of greaseproof paper on top. Cover and cook on low for 4 hours, until firm and the juices are clear, not pink.

5 Turn out the loaf and serve sliced.

HONEY-GLAZED DUCK LEGS

Serves: 4–6　　　**Prep: 15 mins**　　　**Cook: 6 hours 20 mins–10 hours 20 mins**

Ingredients

6 duck legs

125 ml/4 fl oz chicken stock

3 tbsp red wine or white wine

115 g/4 oz clear honey

1 tbsp fresh thyme leaves

salt and pepper

mashed potato or cooked polenta, to serve

Method

1 Trim any excess skin or fat from the duck legs and season to taste with salt and pepper. Heat a large, heavy-based frying pan over a medium–high heat. When the pan is very hot, add the duck legs, in batches, if necessary, and cook on one side for about 4 minutes, until brown. Turn and cook on the other side for about 4 minutes, until brown. Transfer to the slow cooker.

2 Put the stock, wine, honey and thyme into a small bowl, stir to combine, then pour the mixture over the duck legs, turning to coat. Cover and cook on high for about 6 hours or on low for about 10 hours, until the duck is very tender. Serve immediately with mashed potato or polenta.

POULTRY DISHES

CHICKEN ITALIAN-STYLE

Serves: 4 **Prep: 25 mins** **Cook: 5 hours 25 mins–6 hours 25 mins**

Ingredients

1 tbsp plain flour

4 chicken portions, about 175 g/6 oz each

2½ tbsp olive oil

8–12 shallots, halved if large

2–4 garlic cloves, sliced

400 ml/14 fl oz chicken stock

50 ml/2 fl oz dry sherry

4 fresh thyme sprigs

115 g/4 oz cherry tomatoes

115 g/4 oz baby sweetcorn, halved lengthways

2 slices white or wholemeal bread, crusts removed, cubed

salt and pepper

1 tbsp chopped fresh thyme, to garnish

Method

1. Spread out the flour in a shallow dish and season with salt and pepper. Add the chicken portions and toss well to coat, shaking off any excess. Reserve the remaining seasoned flour. Heat 1 tablespoon of the oil in a heavy-based frying pan. Add the chicken portions and cook over a medium–high heat, turning frequently, for 10 minutes until golden brown all over. Using a slotted spoon, transfer the chicken to the slow cooker.

2. Add the shallots and garlic to the frying pan, lower the heat and cook, stirring occasionally, for 5 minutes until softened. Sprinkle in the reserved seasoned flour and cook, stirring constantly, for 2 minutes. Remove from the heat and gradually stir in the stock and sherry, then bring to the boil, stirring constantly. Pour the mixture over the chicken and add the thyme sprigs, tomatoes and baby sweetcorn. Cover and cook on low for 5–6 hours until the chicken is tender and cooked through.

3. Meanwhile, heat the remaining oil in a frying pan, add the bread cubes and cook, stirring frequently, for 4–5 minutes until golden all over. Remove and discard the thyme sprigs from the stew. Serve immediately with the croûtons and garnished with the chopped thyme.

POULTRY DISHES

CHICKEN CACCIATORE

Serves: 4 **Prep: 15 mins** **Cook: 5 hours 25 mins**

Ingredients

3 tbsp olive oil

4 skinless chicken portions

2 onions, sliced

2 garlic cloves, finely chopped

400 g/14 oz canned chopped tomatoes

1 tbsp tomato purée

2 tbsp chopped fresh parsley

2 tsp fresh thyme leaves, plus extra sprigs to garnish

150 ml/5 fl oz red wine

salt and pepper

Method

1 Heat the oil in a heavy-based frying pan. Add the chicken and cook over a medium heat, turning occasionally, for 10 minutes, until golden all over. Using a slotted spoon, transfer the chicken to the slow cooker.

2 Add the onions to the pan and cook, stirring occasionally, for 5 minutes, until softened and just turning golden. Add the garlic, tomatoes, tomato purée, parsley, thyme leaves and wine. Season to taste with salt and pepper and bring to the boil.

3 Pour the tomato mixture over the chicken pieces. Cover and cook on low for 5 hours, until the chicken is tender and cooked through. Taste and adjust the seasoning, if necessary. Transfer to warmed serving plates, garnish with thyme sprigs and serve immediately.

FLORIDA CHICKEN

Serves: 4 **Prep: 30 mins** **Cook: 5 hours 35 mins**

Ingredients

1½ tbsp plain flour

450 g/1 lb skinless, boneless chicken, cut into bite-sized pieces

1 tbsp olive oil

1 onion, cut into wedges

2 celery sticks, sliced

150 ml/5 fl oz orange juice

300 ml/10 fl oz chicken stock

1 tbsp light soy sauce

1–2 tsp clear honey

1 tbsp grated orange rind

1 orange pepper, deseeded and chopped

225 g/8 oz courgettes, halved lengthways and sliced

2 corn cobs, cut into chunks

1 orange, peeled and segmented

salt and pepper

1 tbsp chopped fresh parsley, to garnish

Method

1 Spread out the flour in a shallow dish and season with salt and pepper. Add the chicken and toss well to coat, shaking off any excess. Reserve the remaining seasoned flour.

2 Heat the oil in a heavy-based frying pan. Add the chicken and cook over a high heat, stirring frequently, for 5 minutes until golden brown all over. Using a slotted spoon, transfer the chicken to the slow cooker.

3 Add the onion and celery to the frying pan, lower the heat and cook, stirring occasionally, for 5 minutes until softened. Sprinkle in the reserved seasoned flour and cook, stirring constantly, for 2 minutes. Remove the pan from the heat. Gradually stir in the orange juice, stock, soy sauce and honey, then add the orange rind. Return the pan to the heat and bring to the boil, stirring constantly.

4 Pour the mixture over the chicken and add the orange pepper, courgettes and corn cobs. Cover and cook on low for 5 hours until the chicken is tender and cooked through. Stir in the orange segments, re-cover and cook on high for 15 minutes. Serve immediately garnished with the parsley.

TURKEY & RICE CASSEROLE

Serves: 4   **Prep: 20 mins**   **Cook: 2 hours 5 mins**

Ingredients

1 tbsp olive oil

500 g/1 lb 2 oz diced
turkey breast

1 onion, diced

2 carrots, diced

2 celery sticks, sliced

250 g/9 oz closed-cup
mushrooms, sliced

175 g/6 oz long-grain rice,
preferably basmati

450 ml/16 fl oz hot chicken
stock

salt and pepper

Method

1 Heat the oil in a heavy-based frying pan,
add the turkey and fry over a high heat for
3–4 minutes, until lightly browned.

2 Combine the onion, carrots, celery, mushrooms
and rice in the slow cooker. Arrange the turkey
on top, season well with salt and pepper and
pour the stock over. Cover and cook on high
for 2 hours.

3 Stir lightly with a fork to mix and serve
immediately in warmed bowls.

DUCKLING WITH APPLES

Serves: 6　　　　**Prep: 25 mins**　　　　**Cook: 8½ hours**

Ingredients

1.8–2 kg/4–4 lb 8 oz duckling, cut into 8 pieces

2 tbsp olive oil

1 onion, finely chopped

1 carrot, finely chopped

300 ml/10 fl oz chicken stock

300 ml/10 fl oz dry white wine

bouquet garni

4 eating apples

55 g/2 oz unsalted butter

salt and pepper

Method

1 Season the duckling pieces with salt and pepper. Heat the oil in a large, heavy-based frying pan. Add all the duckling pieces, placing the breast portions skin side down. Cook over a medium–high heat for a few minutes until golden brown, then transfer the breast portions to a plate. Turn the other pieces and continue to cook until browned all over. Transfer to the plate.

2 Add the onion and carrot to the frying pan and cook over a low heat, stirring occasionally, for 5 minutes until the onion is softened. Add the stock and wine and bring to the boil.

3 Transfer the vegetable mixture to the slow cooker. Add the duckling pieces and the bouquet garni. Cover and cook on low for 8 hours, occasionally skimming off the fat from the slow cooker and replacing the lid each time. Shortly before serving, peel, core and slice the apples. Melt the butter in a large frying pan. Add the apple slices and cook over a medium heat, turning occasionally, for 5 minutes until golden.

4 Spoon the cooked apples onto warmed plates and divide the duckling among them. Strain the sauce into a jug and pour it over the duckling. Serve immediately.

PARMESAN CHICKEN

Serves: 4　　　　　　**Prep: 20 mins**　　　　　　**Cook: 4 hours
25 mins**

Ingredients

1 egg, beaten

4 skinless, boneless chicken breasts

85 g/3 oz fine dry breadcrumbs

2 tbsp olive oil

350 g/12 oz ready-made tomato-based pasta sauce

4 thin slices Cheddar cheese

115 g/4 oz finely grated Parmesan cheese

salt and pepper

cooked rice, to serve

Method

1 Season the egg with salt and pepper. Dip each chicken breast in the egg, turning to coat evenly, then dip into the breadcrumbs, lightly pressing down to cover evenly.

2 Heat the oil in a frying pan over a high heat, add the chicken breasts and fry quickly for 3–4 minutes, until golden brown, turning once.

3 Pour the pasta sauce into the slow cooker and place the chicken breasts on top in a single layer. Cover and cook on low for 4 hours.

4 Place a slice of Cheddar cheese on top of each chicken breast and sprinkle with Parmesan cheese. Re-cover and cook on high for a further 20 minutes. Serve immediately with rice.

CHICKEN BRAISED WITH RED CABBAGE

Serves: 4   **Prep: 20–25 mins**   **Cook: 5 hours 20 mins**

Ingredients

2 tbsp sunflower oil

4 skinless chicken thighs or drumsticks

1 onion, chopped

500 g/1 lb 2 oz red cabbage, cored and shredded

2 apples, peeled cored and chopped

12 canned or cooked chestnuts, halved (optional)

½ tsp juniper berries

125 ml/4 fl oz red wine

salt and pepper

fresh flat-leaf parsley, to garnish

Method

1 Heat the oil in a large, heavy-based saucepan. Add the chicken and cook, turning frequently, for 5 minutes until golden on all sides. Using a slotted spoon, transfer to a plate lined with kitchen paper.

2 Add the onion to the saucepan and cook over a medium heat, stirring occasionally, until softened. Stir in the cabbage and apples and cook, stirring occasionally, for 5 minutes. Add the chestnuts, if using, juniper berries and wine and season to taste with salt and pepper. Bring to the boil.

3 Spoon half the cabbage mixture into the slow cooker, add the chicken pieces, then top with the remaining cabbage mixture. Cover and cook on low for 5 hours until the chicken is tender and cooked through. Serve immediately, garnished with the parsley.

MINI CHICKEN POT PIES

Serves: 6

Prep: 30 mins,
plus cooling

**Cook: 4 hours 40 mins–
8 hours 40 mins**

Ingredients

3 tbsp butter

1 onion, diced

115 g/4 oz button
mushrooms, diced

675 g/1 lb 8 oz boneless,
skinless chicken, diced

1 carrot, diced

2 celery sticks, diced

1 tbsp fresh thyme leaves

2 tbsp plain flour

225 ml/8 fl oz milk

175 ml/6 fl oz chicken stock

1 tsp salt

½ tsp pepper

2 sheets ready-rolled
puff pastry

flour, for dusting

Method

1 Melt 1 tablespoon of the butter in a large frying
pan over a medium–high heat. Add the onion
and cook, stirring, for about 5 minutes, until soft.
Add the mushrooms and cook, stirring, for a
further 3 minutes, or until the mushrooms are
beginning to soften. Transfer the mixture to
the slow cooker and add the chicken, carrot,
celery and thyme.

2 Reduce the heat under the frying pan to
medium, add the remaining butter and heat
until melted. Whisk in the flour and cook, whisking
constantly, until the mixture is lightly browned
and begins to give off a nutty aroma. Whisk in
the milk, stock, salt and pepper and continue to
cook, stirring, for a further 5 minutes, or until the
mixture begins to thicken.

3 Add the mixture to the slow cooker and mix well.
Cover and cook on high for about 4 hours or on
low for about 8 hours, until the chicken is tender
and the sauce has thickened. Divide the filling
equally between six 225-g/8-oz ramekins.

4 Preheat the oven to 190°C/375°F/Gas Mark 5. Roll out the pastry on a lightly floured surface and cut out six rounds, each about 2.5 cm/1 inch larger in circumference than the ramekins. Top each filled ramekin with a pastry round, crimping the edges. Prick the pastry on each pie several times with a fork.

5 Place the ramekins on a baking sheet and bake in the preheated oven for about 20 minutes, until the pastry is puffed and golden brown. Leave to cool for about 10 minutes before serving.

SLOW ROAST CHICKEN

Serves: 4-6 **Prep: 15 mins** **Cook: 7 hours**

Ingredients

1.5 kg/3 lb 5 oz oven-ready chicken
½ lemon
1 tbsp olive oil
½ tsp dried thyme
½ tsp paprika
salt and pepper

Method

1 Wipe the chicken with kitchen paper and tuck the lemon half inside the body cavity. Brush the oil over the chicken skin and sprinkle with thyme, paprika and salt and pepper, rubbing in with your fingers to cover all the skin.

2 Place the chicken in the slow cooker, cover and cook on high for 3 hours. Reduce the heat to low and cook for a further 4 hours, until the chicken is tender and cooked through and the juices run clear when a skewer is inserted into the thickest part of the meat.

3 Carefully remove the chicken from the slow cooker and place on a warmed platter. Skim any fat from the juices and spoon over the chicken. Serve immediately.

★ Variation

Create a delicious spice rub by combining 2 teaspoons of paprika, 2 teaspoons of salt, 1 teaspoon each of onion powder, dried thyme and cayenne pepper and ½ teaspoon each of garlic powder and freshly ground black pepper. Rub the spice mixture over the chicken before cooking.

MEAT DISHES

BOSTON BAKED BEANS

Serves: 4–6

Prep: 20 mins,
plus soaking

Cook: 14 hours

Ingredients

450 g/1 lb dried white
haricot beans,
soaked overnight in
cold water and drained

115 g/4 oz salt pork, soaked
in cold water for 3 hours
and drained

3 tbsp black treacle

3 tbsp muscovado sugar

2 tsp dry mustard

1 onion, chopped

salt and pepper

Method

1 Place the beans in the slow cooker and add
about 1.4 litres/2½ pints of boiling water so that
they are covered. Cover and cook the beans
on high for 3 hours. Meanwhile, cut the salt pork
into chunks.

2 Drain the beans, reserving 225 ml/8 fl oz of the
cooking liquid. Mix the reserved liquid with the
treacle, sugar, mustard and 1 teaspoon of salt.

3 Return the beans to the slow cooker and add
the salt pork, onion and the treacle mixture.
Stir, then cover and cook on low for 11 hours.
Serve immediately.

★ **Variation**

Add 1 teaspoon of garlic powder and
2 teaspoons of chilli powder for a little kick to
your beans. You can also add diced peppers for
an extra crunch to this delicious dish.

VIETNAMESE BEEF NOODLE SOUP

Serves: 4　　　　　**Prep: 25 mins**　　　　　**Cook: 5 hours 35 mins– 8 hours 35 mins**

Ingredients

2 litres/3½ pints beef stock

1 onion, quartered

5-cm/2-inch piece of fresh ginger, thickly sliced lengthways

2 cinnamon sticks

3 whole cloves

2 star anise or 1 tsp fennel seeds

2 tbsp Thai fish sauce

1 tsp sugar

450 g/1 lb dried rice noodles

225 g/8 oz top sirloin, very thinly sliced

salt

To serve

115 g/4 oz beansprouts

lime wedges

chopped fresh herbs, including basil, coriander and/or mint

4 spring onions, thinly sliced

2 hot chillies, thinly sliced

Method

1 Put the stock, onion, ginger, cinnamon sticks, cloves, star anise, fish sauce and sugar into the slow cooker and stir to combine. Cover and cook on high for 5 hours or on low for 8 hours. Add salt to taste.

2 Pour the liquid through a fine-meshed sieve or a colander lined with muslin and discard the solids. Return the clear stock to the slow cooker and heat on high for about 30 minutes, until very hot, or transfer to a large saucepan and bring to a slow boil over a medium–high heat.

3 Just before serving, cook the noodles according to the packet instructions.

4 Place a few slices of beef in the base of each of four soup bowls and ladle the hot soup over to lightly cook the beef. Add some noodles to each bowl. Serve immediately with the beansprouts, lime wedges, herbs, spring onions and chillies in separate bowls for diners to help themselves.

MEAT DISHES

MANGO BEEF IN LETTUCE CUPS

Serves: 6–8   **Prep: 20 mins**   **Cook: 2 hours**

Ingredients

675 g/1 lb 8 oz chuck steak, cut into 1-cm/½-inch dice

1 tbsp cornflour

1 fresh mango, peeled, stoned and diced

2 hot red chillies, deseeded and diced

2 tbsp soy sauce

2 tbsp mirin or other sweet white wine

2 tbsp brown sugar

1 tsp sesame oil

cup-shaped lettuce leaves, to serve

Method

1 Put the beef and the cornflour into the slow cooker and toss to coat the beef evenly. Add the mango and chillies and stir to mix. Add the soy sauce, mirin, sugar and oil and stir to mix well.

2 Cover and cook on high for about 1 hour, then set the lid slightly ajar and continue to cook on high for a further 1 hour, until the meat is tender and the sauce has thickened.

3 Transfer the meat to a serving bowl and serve with the lettuce leaves, so that diners can scoop some of the meat into a lettuce cup and wrap it up like a taco.

PORK VINDALOO

Serves: 6

Prep: 25 mins,
plus marinating

**Cook: 8 hours 10 mins–
9 hours 10 mins**

Ingredients

1 tsp cumin seeds

½–1 tsp black mustard
seeds

1 tsp fenugreek seeds

1 tsp black peppercorns

4–6 dried red chillies

6 tbsp white wine vinegar

1 kg/2 lb 4 oz diced pork

300 g/10½ oz tomatoes,
peeled and chopped

1 onion, sliced

2 garlic cloves,
finely chopped

1 green pepper, deseeded
and chopped

1 tbsp groundnut oil

1 tsp ground cinnamon

½ tsp ground turmeric

juice and grated rind of
1 lime

2.5-cm/1-inch piece fresh
ginger, finely chopped

500 ml/18 fl oz water

4 tbsp chopped
fresh coriander

salt and pepper

cooked rice, to serve

Method

1 Put the cumin, mustard and fenugreek seeds, peppercorns and dried chillies into a spice grinder or mortar and grind to a powder. Transfer to a large non-metallic bowl and stir in the vinegar and ½ teaspoon of salt. Add the pork, tomatoes, onion, garlic, green pepper, oil, cinnamon, turmeric, lime juice and rind and ginger and mix well. Cover with clingfilm and leave to marinate overnight in the refrigerator.

2 Transfer the mixture to a large saucepan, pour in the water and bring to the boil, stirring frequently. Transfer to the slow cooker, cover and cook on low for 8–9 hours, until the meat is tender.

3 Taste and adjust the seasoning, adding salt and pepper if needed. Stir in the chopped coriander and serve immediately with rice.

KOREAN BRAISED BEEF RIBS

Serves: 4–6 **Prep: 20 mins,** **Cook: 6–9 hours**
plus marinating

Ingredients

1 onion, diced

3 garlic cloves,
finely chopped

1 tbsp finely chopped
fresh ginger

2 tbsp soy sauce

2 tbsp soft dark brown sugar

2 tbsp mirin or other sweet
white wine

1 tbsp sesame oil

1 tsp chilli paste

1.25 kg/2 lb 12 oz bone-in
beef short ribs

2 small potatoes, cubed

2 carrots, cubed

3 spring onions, thinly sliced,
to garnish

1 tbsp toasted sesame
seeds, to garnish

steamed rice, to serve

Method

1 Put the onion, garlic, ginger, soy sauce, sugar, mirin, oil and chilli paste into a bowl large enough to hold the meat and stir to combine. Add the ribs and turn to coat in the mixture. Cover and place in the refrigerator to marinate for at least 2 hours or overnight.

2 Place the beef, together with the marinade, in the slow cooker. Add the potatoes and carrots and stir to mix. Cover and cook on high for about 6 hours or on low for about 9 hours, until the meat is tender and falling off the bone.

3 Serve immediately with freshly cooked rice and garnished with spring onions and sesame seeds.

PORK WITH PEPPERS

Serves: 4　　　　**Prep: 20 mins**　　　　**Cook: 8 hours 20 mins–9 hours 20 mins**

Ingredients

2 tbsp olive oil

4 pork chops, trimmed of excess fat

1 shallot, chopped

2 garlic cloves, finely chopped

2 orange peppers, deseeded and sliced

1 tbsp plain flour

600 ml/1 pint chicken stock

1 tbsp medium–hot Indian curry paste

115 g/4 oz ready-to-eat dried apricots

salt and pepper

baby spinach leaves and cooked couscous, to serve

Method

1　Heat the oil in a large frying pan. Add the chops and cook over a medium heat for 2–4 minutes on each side, until evenly browned. Remove with tongs and put them into the slow cooker.

2　Add the shallot, garlic and peppers to the pan, reduce the heat and cook, stirring occasionally, for 5 minutes, until softened. Stir in the flour and cook, stirring constantly, for 1 minute. Gradually stir in the stock, a little at a time, then add the curry paste and apricots. Bring to the boil, stirring occasionally.

3　Season to taste with salt and pepper and transfer the mixture to the slow cooker. Cover and cook on low for 8–9 hours, until the meat is tender. Serve immediately with baby spinach and couscous.

MEAT DISHES

MEXICAN PORK CHOPS

Serves: 4   **Prep: 20 mins**   **Cook: 6½ hours**

Ingredients

4 pork chops, trimmed of excess fat

2 tbsp corn oil

450 g/1 lb canned pineapple chunks in juice

1 red pepper, deseeded and finely chopped

2 fresh jalapeño chillies, deseeded and finely chopped

1 onion, finely chopped

1 tbsp chopped fresh coriander, plus extra sprigs to garnish

125 ml/4 fl oz hot chicken stock

salt and pepper

flour tortillas, to serve

Method

1 Season the chops with salt and pepper to taste. Heat the oil in a large heavy-based frying pan. Add the chops and cook over a medium heat for 2–3 minutes on each side, until lightly browned. Transfer them to the slow cooker. Drain the pineapple, reserving the juice, and set aside.

2 Add the red pepper, chillies and onion to the frying pan and cook, stirring occasionally, for 5 minutes, until the onion is softened. Transfer the mixture to the slow cooker and add the chopped coriander, stock and 125 ml/4 fl oz of the reserved pineapple juice. Cover and cook on low for 6 hours, until the chops are tender.

3 Add the pineapple chunks to the slow cooker, re-cover and cook on high for 15 minutes. Garnish with coriander sprigs and serve immediately with flour tortillas.

MEAT DISHES

BEEF & CHIPOTLE BURRITOS

Serves: 4

Prep: 25 mins,
plus soaking

**Cook: 4 hours
10 mins**

Ingredients

1 tbsp olive oil

1 onion, sliced

600 g/1 lb 5 oz chuck steak

1 dried chipotle pepper,
soaked in boiling water
for 20 minutes

1 garlic clove, crushed

1 tsp ground cumin

400 g/14 oz canned
chopped tomatoes

8 large tortillas

salt and pepper

soured cream and green
salad, to serve

Method

1 Heat the oil in a pan and fry the onion for
3–4 minutes until golden. Tip into the slow cooker
and arrange the beef on top. Drain and chop
the chipotle. Sprinkle the chopped chipotle,
garlic, cumin, tomatoes, salt and pepper over
the meat.

2 Cover and cook on low for 4 hours, until the
meat is tender.

3 Warm the tortillas according to the packet
instructions. Remove the beef and shred with a
fork. Divide between the tortillas and spoon over
the sauce. Wrap, and serve with soured cream
and green salad.

BEEF ROULADES WITH SPINACH & FETA CHEESE

Serves: 4   **Prep: 20 mins**   **Cook: 3–6 hours**

Ingredients

4 chuck steaks, about
675 g/1 lb 8 oz in total,
pounded to a thickness of
1 cm/½ inch

½ onion, diced

115 g/4 oz feta cheese,
crumbled

30 g/1 oz stoned Kalamata
olives, chopped

4 small handfuls baby
spinach leaves

50 ml/2 fl oz beef
stock or water

salt and pepper

Method

1 Season the steaks on both sides with salt and pepper. Top each steak with a quarter each of the onion, cheese, olives and spinach. Starting with one of the short sides, roll up the steaks into pinwheels and secure with kitchen string or wooden cocktail sticks.

2 Place the steak rolls in the slow cooker along with the stock, cover, and cook on high for about 3 hours or on low for 6 hours, until the meat is tender and cooked through. Serve immediately.

PORK & VEGETABLE RAGOUT

Serves: 4

Prep: 30 mins

**Cook: 5 hours 20 mins–
6 hours 20 mins**

Ingredients

450 g/1 lb lean,
boneless pork

1½ tbsp plain flour

1 tsp ground coriander

1 tsp ground cumin

1½ tsp ground cinnamon

1 tbsp olive oil

1 onion, chopped

400 g/14 oz canned
chopped tomatoes

2 tbsp tomato purée

300 ml/10 fl oz chicken
stock

225 g/8 oz carrots, chopped

350 g/12 oz squash, such as
kabocha, peeled,
deseeded and chopped

225 g/8 oz leeks, sliced,
blanched and drained

115 g/4 oz okra,
trimmed and sliced

salt and pepper

sprigs of fresh parsley,
to garnish

couscous, to serve

Method

1 Trim off any visible fat from the pork and cut the meat into thin strips about 5 cm/2 inches long. Mix together the flour, coriander, cumin and cinnamon in a shallow dish, add the pork strips and toss well to coat. Shake off the excess and reserve the remaining spiced flour.

2 Heat the oil in a heavy-based frying pan. Add the onion and cook over a low heat, stirring occasionally, for 5 minutes until softened. Add the pork strips, increase the heat to high and cook, stirring frequently, for 5 minutes until browned all over. Sprinkle in the reserved spiced flour and cook, stirring constantly, for 2 minutes, then remove the pan from the heat.

3 Gradually stir in the tomatoes with their can juices. Combine the tomato purée with the stock in a jug, then gradually stir the mixture into the frying pan. Add the carrots, return the pan to the heat and bring to the boil, stirring constantly.

4 Transfer to the slow cooker, stir in the squash, leeks and okra, and season to taste with salt and pepper. Cover and cook on low for 5–6 hours until the meat and vegetables are tender. Garnish with parsley sprigs and serve immediately with couscous.

HAM COOKED IN CIDER

Serves: 6 **Prep: 20 mins** **Cook: 8 hours,**
plus standing

Ingredients

1 kg/2 lb 4 oz boneless
gammon joint

1 onion, halved

4 cloves

6 black peppercorns

1 tsp juniper berries

1 celery stick, chopped

1 carrot, sliced

1 litre/1¾ pints medium
cider

fresh salad, to serve

Method

1 Place a trivet or rack in the slow cooker, if you
like, and stand the gammon on it. Otherwise,
just place the gammon in the slow cooker. Stud
each onion half with two of the cloves and add
to the slow cooker with the peppercorns, juniper
berries, celery and carrot.

2 Pour in the cider, cover and cook on low for
8 hours, until the meat is tender.

3 Remove the gammon from the cooker and
place on a board. Tent with foil and leave to
stand for 10–15 minutes. Discard the cooking
liquid and flavourings.

4 Cut off any rind and fat from the gammon joint
and carve into slices. Transfer to serving plates
and serve immediately with a fresh salad.

BEEF RAGÙ WITH TAGLIATELLE

Serves: 6   **Prep: 20 mins**   **Cook: 8 hours 25 mins–8 hours 55 mins**

Ingredients

3 tbsp olive oil

85 g/3 oz pancetta, diced

1 onion, chopped

1 garlic clove, finely chopped

1 carrot, chopped

1 celery stick, chopped

450 g/1 lb minced steak

125 ml/4 fl oz red wine

2 tbsp tomato purée

400 g/14 oz canned chopped tomatoes

300 ml/10 fl oz beef stock

½ tsp dried oregano

450 g/1 lb dried tagliatelle

salt and pepper

grated Parmesan cheese, to serve

Method

1 Heat the oil in a saucepan. Add the pancetta and cook over a medium heat, stirring frequently, for 3 minutes. Reduce the heat, add the onion, garlic, carrot and celery and cook, stirring occasionally, for 5 minutes, until the vegetables have softened.

2 Increase the heat to medium and add the minced steak. Cook, stirring frequently and breaking it up with a wooden spoon, for 8–10 minutes, until evenly browned. Pour in the wine and cook for a few minutes, until the alcohol has evaporated, then stir in the tomato purée, tomatoes, stock and oregano and season to taste with salt and pepper.

3 Bring to the boil, then transfer the ragù to the slow cooker. Cover and cook on low for 8–8½ hours.

4 Shortly before serving, bring a large saucepan of lightly salted water to the boil. Add the pasta, bring back to the boil and cook for 8–10 minutes, until tender but still firm to the bite. Drain and tip into a warmed serving bowl. Add the ragù to the pasta. Toss with two forks, sprinkle with the Parmesan and serve immediately.

MEAT DISHES

CHINESE-STYLE BARBECUE PORK

Serves: 4-6

Prep: 20 mins, plus marinating

Cook: 6-10 hours

Ingredients

2 garlic cloves, finely chopped

1 tbsp finely chopped fresh ginger

2 tbsp honey

2 tbsp soy sauce

2 tbsp mirin or other sweet white wine

1 tsp sesame oil

1 tsp Chinese five-spice powder

900 g/2 lb pork shoulder, boned and rolled

3 spring onions, thinly sliced, to garnish

steamed rice, to serve

Method

1 Put the garlic, ginger, honey, soy sauce, mirin, oil and five-spice powder into a large bowl and stir to mix. Add the pork and stir to coat. Cover and refrigerate for at least 2 hours or overnight.

2 Place the pork and the marinade in the slow cooker. Cover and cook on high for 6 hours or on low for 10 hours, until the meat is very tender.

3 Slice the meat and then pull into shreds using two forks. Garnish with spring onions and serve immediately with freshly cooked rice.

MEAT DISHES

BEEF IN BEER

Serves: 4–6

Prep: 20 mins

Cook: 8 hours 35 mins–9 hours 35 mins

Ingredients

4 tbsp sunflower oil

1 kg/2 lb 4 oz topside of beef, in one piece

1.5 kg/3 lb 5 oz red onions, thinly sliced

500 ml/18 fl oz beef stock

1½ tbsp plain flour

350 ml/12 fl oz beer

3 garlic cloves, chopped

1 strip thinly pared lemon rind

1 bay leaf

2 tbsp molasses

salt and pepper

fresh flat-leaf parsley sprigs, to garnish

Method

1 Heat the oil in a large frying pan. Add the beef and cook over a medium–high heat, turning occasionally, for 5–8 minutes, until evenly browned. Transfer the beef to the slow cooker.

2 Reduce the heat to low and add the onions to the pan. Cook, stirring occasionally, for 5 minutes, until softened. Stir in 2 tablespoons of the stock, scraping up the sediment from the base of the pan, and cook until all the liquid has evaporated. Add another 2 tablespoons of the stock and continue to cook for a further 15 minutes, adding 2 tablespoons of the stock each time the previous addition has evaporated.

3 Stir in the flour and cook, stirring constantly, for 1 minute, then gradually stir in the remaining stock and the beer. Increase the heat to medium and bring to the boil, stirring constantly.

4 Stir in the garlic, lemon rind, bay leaf and molasses and season to taste with salt and pepper. Transfer the onion mixture to the slow cooker, cover and cook on low for 8–9 hours, until the beef is cooked to your liking. Remove and discard the bay leaf and serve immediately, garnished with parsley sprigs.

MEAT DISHES

BEEF & BUTTON ONIONS

Serves: 4–6   **Prep: 20 mins**   **Cook: 9¼ hours**

Ingredients

2 tbsp olive oil

450 g/1 lb button onions, peeled but left whole

2 garlic cloves, halved

900 g/2 lb stewing beef, cubed

½ tsp ground cinnamon

1 tsp ground cloves

1 tsp ground cumin

2 tbsp tomato purée

75 cl bottle red wine

grated rind and juice of 1 orange

1 bay leaf

salt and pepper

1 tbsp chopped fresh flat-leaf parsley, to garnish

mashed potato, to serve

Method

1 Heat the oil in a heavy-based frying pan. Add the onions and garlic and cook over a medium heat, stirring frequently, for 5 minutes until softened and beginning to brown. Increase the heat to high, add the beef and cook, stirring frequently, for 5 minutes, until browned all over.

2 Stir in the cinnamon, cloves, cumin and tomato purée and season to taste with salt and pepper. Pour in the wine, scraping up any sediment from the base of the frying pan. Stir in the orange rind and juice, add the bay leaf and bring to the boil.

3 Transfer the mixture to the slow cooker, cover and cook on low for 9 hours, until the beef is tender. If possible, stir the stew once during the second half of the cooking time.

4 Remove and discard the bay leaf and serve the stew immediately, garnished with the parsley and accompanied by mashed potato.

MEAT DISHES

MOROCCAN SPICED BEEF STEW

Serves: 4–6　　**Prep: 20 mins**　　**Cook: 6 hours 10 mins–9 hours 10 mins**

Ingredients

2 tbsp vegetable oil

1 onion, diced

1½ tsp salt

½ tsp pepper

2 tsp ground cumin

½ tsp ground cinnamon

½ tsp ground ginger

225 ml/8 fl oz red wine

675 g/1 lb 8 oz chuck steak, cut into 5-cm/2-inch pieces

130 g/4¾ oz dried apricots, diced

2 tbsp honey

125 ml/4 fl oz water

chopped fresh coriander, to garnish

cooked couscous, to serve

Method

1　Heat the oil in a large frying pan. Add the onion and cook, stirring, for about 5 minutes, until soft. Add the salt, pepper, cumin, cinnamon and ginger and cook, stirring, for a further 1 minute.

2　Add the wine, bring to the boil and cook for 1 minute, scraping up any sediment from the base of the pan. Transfer the mixture to the slow cooker.

3　Add the beef, apricots, honey and water and stir to mix. Cover and cook on high for 6 hours or on low for 9 hours, until the meat is very tender.

4　Serve immediately with couscous, garnished with coriander.

SPICY PULLED PORK

Serves: 4　　　　**Prep: 25 mins**　　　　**Cook: 8 hours**

Ingredients

2 onions, sliced

1.5 kg/3 lb 5 oz boned and
rolled pork shoulder

2 tbsp demerara sugar

2 tbsp Worcestershire sauce

1 tbsp American mustard

2 tbsp tomato ketchup

1 tbsp cider vinegar

salt and pepper

burger buns or ciabatta
rolls, to serve

Method

1 Put the onions in the slow cooker and place the pork on top. Mix the sugar, Worcestershire sauce, mustard, ketchup and vinegar together and spread all over the surface of the pork. Season to taste with salt and pepper. Cover and cook on low for 8 hours.

2 Remove the pork from the slow cooker and use two forks to pull it apart into shreds.

3 Skim any excess fat from the juices and stir a little juice into the pork. Serve in burger buns, with the remaining juices for spooning over.

SHREDDED BEEF WITH TZATZIKI SAUCE

Serves: 4   **Prep: 30 mins**   **Cook: 5–9 hours**

Ingredients

3 tbsp natural yogurt

1 tbsp lemon juice

2 garlic cloves, finely chopped

1 tsp crumbled dried oregano or 1 tbsp chopped fresh oregano

¾ tsp salt

½ tsp pepper

675 g/1 lb 8 oz chuck steak, diced

Sauce

1 cucumber, peeled, deseeded and coarsely grated

1 tsp salt

225 ml/8 fl oz natural yogurt

3 tbsp lemon juice

50 g/1¾ oz chopped fresh mint leaves

To serve

4 rounds warmed flatbread or pitta

1 large tomato, cut into wedges

115 g/4 oz shredded lettuce

Method

1 Put the yogurt, lemon juice, garlic, oregano, salt and pepper into the slow cooker and stir to mix well. Add the beef and turn to coat. Cover and cook on high for about 5 hours or on low for about 9 hours, until the beef is tender. Shred the beef with a fork and mix it with the cooking juices.

2 To make the sauce, place the cucumber on a double layer of kitchen paper and sprinkle with ½ teaspoon of the salt. Set aside. Put the yogurt, the remaining salt, lemon juice and mint into a medium-sized bowl and stir to combine. Wrap the cucumber in the kitchen paper and squeeze out the excess juice over the sink. Mix the cucumber into the yogurt mixture.

3 Serve the shredded beef on flatbread, drizzled with the sauce and topped with tomato wedges and shredded lettuce.

MEAT DISHES

THAI BEEF CURRY

Serves: 4   **Prep: 20 mins**   **Cook: 5–9 hours**

Ingredients

75 g/2¾ oz Thai red curry paste

175 ml/6 fl oz unsweetened coconut milk

50 g/1¾ oz soft dark brown sugar

1 tbsp Thai fish sauce

75 g/2¾ oz smooth peanut butter

900 g/2 lb chuck steak, cut into 2.5-cm/1-inch dice

2 potatoes, diced

125 ml/4 fl oz beef stock or water

fresh basil leaves, cut into ribbons, to garnish

steamed rice, to serve

Method

1 Put the curry paste, coconut milk, sugar, fish sauce and peanut butter into the slow cooker and stir to combine. Add the beef, potatoes and stock and stir to coat in the mixture.

2 Cover and cook on high for about 4 hours or on low for 8 hours, then set the lid slightly ajar and cook for a further 1 hour, or until the beef is very tender and the sauce has thickened slightly. Serve immediately, garnished with basil and accompanied with the steamed rice.

BEEF EMPANADAS

Makes: about 30

Prep: 35 mins, plus cooling

Cook: 4 hours 35 mins

Ingredients

1 tbsp vegetable oil

1 onion, finely chopped

1 garlic clove, finely chopped

450 g/1lb extra lean fresh beef mince

1 tsp salt

1 tsp ground cumin

1 tsp chilli powder

1 tsp dried oregano or 1 tbsp finely chopped fresh oregano

1 red pepper, deseeded and sliced

70 g/2½ oz pimiento-stuffed green olives, chopped

40 g/1½ oz sultanas

2 tbsp tomato purée

450 g/1 lb ready-made shortcrust pastry

flour for dusting

Method

1 Heat the oil in a large frying pan over a medium–high heat. Add the onion and garlic and cook, stirring, for about 5 minutes, until soft. Add the beef and cook, stirring, until brown. Drain off the excess fat and discard. Add the salt, cumin, chilli powder and oregano and continue to cook, stirring, for a further minute, then transfer to the slow cooker.

2 Add the red pepper, olives, sultanas and tomato purée and stir to combine. Cover and cook on low for 4 hours.

3 Preheat the oven to 200°C/400°F/Gas Mark 6 and line a baking tray with baking paper. Roll out the pastry on a lightly floured surface and cut it into 6-cm/2½ -inch rounds with a pastry cutter. Place about 1 tablespoon of the filling on each round, fold over the pastry and crimp the edges together to seal each pie.

4 Place the finished empanadas on the prepared baking tray and bake in the preheated oven for 20–25 minutes, until golden brown. Remove from the oven and transfer to a wire rack to cool slightly. Serve warm.

PORK STUFFED WITH APPLES

Serves: 4　　　　**Prep: 25 mins**　　　　**Cook: 4–7 hours**

Ingredients

1 large apple, peeled, cored and sliced

125 ml/4 fl oz apple juice or water

4 boneless pork chops, about 2.5 cm/1 inch thick

4 slices prosciutto

115 g/4 oz Gorgonzola cheese

salt and pepper

mashed potato, to serve

Method

1 Place half of the apple slices in the base of the slow cooker and add the apple juice.

2 Butterfly the pork chops by laying each chop flat on a chopping board and, pressing down on it with the flat of your hand to keep it in place, cutting through the centre horizontally, leaving one side attached like a hinge. Loosely wrap in clingfilm and gently pound with a meat mallet to a thickness of about 2 cm/¾ inch.

3 Open the flattened and butterflied chops like books and place on the chopping board. Layer each chop with a slice of prosciutto, a quarter of the cheese and a quarter of the remaining apple slices. Fold closed and secure with wooden cocktail sticks.

4 Season the stuffed chops all over with salt and pepper and place in the slow cooker on top of the apple slices. Cover and cook on high for about 4 hours or on low for about 7 hours, until the meat is cooked through. Serve immediately with mashed potato.

BEEF STEW

Serves: 6　　　**Prep: 25 mins**　　　**Cook: 8½–9½ hours**

Ingredients

4 tbsp plain flour

1 kg/2 lb 4 oz braising steak, cut into 4-cm/1½-inch cubes

2 tbsp sunflower oil

85 g/3 oz bacon, diced

55 g/2 oz butter

2 onions, thinly sliced

4 carrots, sliced

600 g/1 lb 5 oz potatoes, cut into chunks

115 g/4 oz mushrooms, sliced

1 bay leaf

2 fresh thyme sprigs, finely chopped, plus extra sprigs to garnish

1 tbsp finely chopped fresh parsley

400 g/14 oz canned chopped tomatoes

350 ml/12 fl oz beef stock

salt and pepper

Method

1　Put the flour into a polythene bag and season to taste with salt and pepper. Add the steak cubes, in batches, hold the top securely and shake well to coat. Transfer the meat to a plate.

2　Heat the oil in a large frying pan. Add the bacon and cook over a low heat, stirring frequently, for 5 minutes. Add the steak cubes, increase the heat to medium and cook, stirring frequently, for 8–10 minutes, until evenly browned. Remove the meat with a slotted spoon and set aside on a plate.

3　Wipe out the pan with kitchen paper, then return to a low heat and melt the butter. Add the onions and cook, stirring occasionally, for 5 minutes, until softened. Add the carrots, potatoes and mushrooms and cook, stirring occasionally, for a further 5 minutes.

4　Season to taste with salt and pepper, add the bay leaf, chopped thyme, parsley and tomatoes and pour in the stock. Bring to the boil, stirring occasionally, then remove the pan from the heat and transfer the mixture to the slow cooker. Stir in the meat, cover and cook on low for 8–9 hours. Remove and discard the bay leaf. Garnish with thyme sprigs and serve immediately.

BEEF RIBS BRAISED IN RED WINE

Serves: 6   **Prep: 20 mins**   **Cook: 7 hours 35 mins–10 hours 35 mins**

Ingredients

1.3 kg/3 lb bone-in beef short ribs

2 tbsp vegetable oil, plus extra, if needed

1 onion, diced

1 celery stick, diced

1 carrot, diced

1 tbsp tomato purée

3 fresh thyme sprigs

2 garlic cloves, finely chopped

3 tbsp plain flour

450 ml/16 fl oz red wine

225 ml/8 fl oz beef stock

1 bay leaf

salt and pepper

mashed potato or cooked polenta, to serve

Method

1 Generously season the ribs with salt and pepper. Heat the oil in a large, heavy-based frying pan over a medium–high heat. Add the ribs and cook, turning occasionally, for about 10 minutes, until brown on all sides. Transfer to the slow cooker.

2 Add more oil to the pan if needed and, when hot, add the onion, celery and carrot to the pan. Cook, stirring occasionally, for about 15 minutes, until the vegetables are soft. Add the tomato purée, thyme, garlic and flour and cook, stirring, for a further 1 minute.

3 Add the wine, bring to the boil and cook for a further 1–2 minutes, stirring and scraping up any sediment from the base of the pan. Reduce the heat to medium–low and simmer for 6–8 minutes, until the liquid is reduced by about half. Transfer to the slow cooker.

4 Stir in the stock, ½ teaspoon of salt and the bay leaf, cover and cook on high for 7 hours or on low for 10 hours, until the meat is very tender and falling from the bone. About 1–2 hours before the end of cooking, set the lid ajar to allow the liquid to reduce and thicken.

5 Remove and discard the thyme and bay leaf and serve with the mashed potato.

MEAT DISHES

PORK WITH ALMONDS

Serves: 4   **Prep: 20 mins**   **Cook: 5½ hours–
5 hours 40 mins**

Ingredients

2 tbsp corn oil or sunflower oil

2 onions, chopped

2 garlic cloves, finely chopped

5-cm/2-inch cinnamon stick

3 cloves

115 g/4 oz ground almonds

750 g/1 lb 10 oz boneless pork, cut into 2.5-cm/1-inch cubes

4 tomatoes, peeled and chopped

2 tbsp capers

115 g/4 oz green olives, stoned

3 pickled jalapeño chillies, drained, deseeded and cut into rings

350 ml/12 fl oz chicken stock

salt and pepper

Method

1 Heat half the oil in a large heavy-based frying pan. Add the onions and cook over a low heat, stirring occasionally, for 5 minutes, until softened. Add the garlic, cinnamon stick, cloves and almonds and cook, stirring frequently, for 8–10 minutes. Be careful not to burn the almonds.

2 Remove and discard the cinnamon stick and cloves and transfer the mixture to a food processor. Process to a smooth purée.

3 Wipe out the pan with kitchen paper, then return to the heat. Heat the remaining oil, then add the pork, in batches if necessary. Cook over a medium heat, stirring frequently, for 5–10 minutes, until evenly browned.

4 Add the almond purée, tomatoes, capers, olives, chillies and stock to the pan. Bring to the boil, then transfer to the slow cooker. Season to taste with salt and pepper and mix well. Cover and cook on low for 5 hours until the meat is cooked through and no traces of pink remain. Transfer to warmed plates and serve immediately.

MEAT DISHES

RED-COOKED BEEF

Serves: 6

Prep: 20 mins,
plus soaking

Cook: 9–9¼ hours

Ingredients

4 dried Chinese wood ear mushrooms

4 tbsp groundnut oil

1 kg/2 lb 4 oz topside of beef, cut into 2.5-cm/ 1-inch cubes

3 tbsp dark soy sauce

2 tbsp Chinese rice wine or dry sherry

1 tbsp tomato purée

2.5-cm/1-inch piece fresh ginger, very finely chopped

2 garlic cloves, very finely chopped

2 tbsp soft light brown sugar

1 tsp Chinese five-spice powder

700 ml/1¼ pints beef stock

280 g/10 oz carrots, thinly sliced diagonally

cooked egg noodles, to serve

Method

1 Put the mushrooms into a heatproof bowl and pour in warm water to cover. Set aside to soak for 20 minutes.

2 Meanwhile, heat the oil in a large saucepan. Add the beef, in batches, and cook over a medium heat, stirring frequently, for 8–10 minutes, until evenly browned. Remove with a slotted spoon and drain on kitchen paper.

3 Drain the mushrooms, discarding the soaking water, and gently squeeze out any excess liquid. Cut off and discard the stems, slice the caps and put them into a bowl. Add the soy sauce, rice wine, tomato purée, ginger, garlic, sugar, five-spice powder and stock and mix well.

4 When all the meat has been browned, wipe out the pan with kitchen paper. Return the meat to the pan, stir in the mushroom mixture and bring to the boil.

5 Transfer the mixture to the slow cooker, cover and cook on low for 8 hours, until the meat is tender. Stir in the carrots, re-cover and cook on high for a further 45–60 minutes, until the carrots are tender. Serve immediately with noodles.

CHUNKY BEEF CHILLI

Serves: 4

Prep: 20 mins,
plus soaking

Cook: 9¼ hours

Ingredients

250 g/9 oz dried red kidney beans, soaked overnight

600 ml/1 pint water

2 garlic cloves, chopped

5 tbsp tomato purée

1 small green chilli, chopped

2 tsp ground cumin

2 tsp ground coriander

600 g/1 lb 5 oz chuck steak, diced

1 large onion, chopped

1 large green pepper, deseeded and sliced

salt and pepper

soured cream, to serve

Method

1 Drain and rinse the beans, place in a saucepan, add enough water to cover and bring to a boil. Boil rapidly for 10 minutes, then remove from the heat and drain and rinse again. Place the beans in the slow cooker and add 600 ml/1 pint of cold water.

2 Mix the garlic, tomato purée, chilli, cumin and coriander together in a large bowl. Add the steak, onion and green pepper and mix to coat evenly.

3 Place the meat and vegetables on top of the beans, cover and cook on low for 9 hours, until the beans and meat are tender. Stir and season to taste with salt and pepper.

4 Transfer to warmed serving bowls and top with a swirl of soured cream. Serve immediately.

BEEF & VEGETABLE STEW WITH CORN

Serves: 4　　　　**Prep: 25 mins**　　　　**Cook: 9½ hours**

Ingredients

1½ tbsp plain flour

1 tsp hot paprika

1–1½ tsp chilli powder

1 tsp ground ginger

450 g/1 lb stewing steak, cubed

2 tbsp olive oil

1 large onion, cut into chunks

3 garlic cloves, sliced

2 celery sticks, sliced

225 g/8 oz carrots, chopped

300 ml/10 fl oz lager

300 ml/10 fl oz beef stock

350 g/12 oz potatoes, chopped

2 corn cobs, halved

1 red pepper, deseeded and chopped

115 g/4 oz tomatoes, cut into quarters

115 g/4 oz shelled peas, thawed if frozen

1 tbsp chopped fresh coriander

salt and pepper

Method

1 Combine the flour, paprika, chilli powder and ginger in a shallow dish, add the steak cubes and toss well to coat. Shake off any excess.

2 Heat the oil in a heavy-based frying pan. Add the onion, garlic and celery and cook over a low heat, stirring occasionally, for 5 minutes, until softened. Increase the heat to high, add the steak and cook, stirring frequently, for 3 minutes until browned all over. Add the carrots and remove the pan from the heat.

3 Gradually stir in the lager and stock, return the frying pan to the heat and bring to the boil, stirring constantly. Transfer the mixture to the slow cooker, add the potatoes and corn cobs, cover and cook on low for 8½ hours.

4 Add the red pepper, tomatoes and peas, re-cover and cook on high for 45 minutes, until the meat is tender and the vegetables are cooked through. Taste and adjust the seasoning if necessary, sprinkle with the coriander and serve immediately.

LAMB WITH SPRING VEGETABLES

Serves: 4–6   **Prep: 25 mins**   **Cook: 9–11 hours**

Ingredients

5 tbsp olive oil

6 shallots, chopped

1 garlic clove, chopped

2 celery sticks, chopped

2 tbsp plain flour

700 g/1 lb 9 oz boned leg or shoulder of lamb, cut into 2.5-cm/1-inch cubes

850 ml/1½ pints chicken stock

115 g/4 oz pearl barley, rinsed

225 g/8 oz small turnips, halved

225 g/8 oz baby carrots

225 g/8 oz frozen petits pois, thawed

225 g/8 oz frozen baby broad beans, thawed

salt and pepper

chopped fresh parsley, to garnish

Method

1 Heat 3 tablespoons of the oil in a large saucepan. Add the shallots, garlic and celery and cook over a low heat, stirring occasionally, for 8–10 minutes, until softened and lightly browned.

2 Meanwhile, put the flour into a polythene bag and season well with salt and pepper. Add the lamb cubes, in batches, and shake well to coat. Transfer the meat to a plate.

3 Using a slotted spoon, transfer the vegetables to the slow cooker. Add the remaining oil to the pan. Add the lamb, in batches if necessary, increase the heat to medium and cook, stirring frequently, for 8–10 minutes, until evenly browned.

4 Return all the lamb to the pan. Gradually stir in the stock, scraping up the sediment from the base of the pan. Stir in the pearl barley, turnips and carrots, season to taste with salt and pepper and bring to the boil. Transfer the mixture to the slow cooker and stir well. Cover and cook on low for 8–10 hours, until the lamb is tender.

5 Sprinkle the petits pois and broad beans on top of the stew, re-cover and cook for another 30 minutes. Stir well, garnish with the parsley and serve immediately.

GOULASH

Serves: 4

Prep: 20 mins

Cook: 9 hours 25 mins

Ingredients

4 tbsp sunflower oil

650 g/1 lb 7 oz braising steak, cut into 2.5-cm/ 1-inch cubes

2 tsp plain flour

2 tsp paprika

300 ml/10 fl oz beef stock

3 onions, chopped

4 carrots, diced

1 large potato or 2 medium potatoes, diced

1 bay leaf

½–1 tsp caraway seeds

400 g/14 oz canned chopped tomatoes

2 tbsp soured cream

salt and pepper

Method

1 Heat half the oil in a heavy-based frying pan. Add the beef and cook over a medium heat, stirring frequently, until browned all over. Lower the heat and stir in the flour and paprika. Cook, stirring constantly, for 2 minutes. Gradually stir in the stock and bring to the boil, then transfer the mixture to the slow cooker.

2 Rinse out the frying pan and heat the remaining oil in it. Add the onions and cook over a low heat, stirring occasionally, for 5 minutes until softened. Stir in the carrots and potato and cook for a few minutes more. Add the bay leaf, caraway seeds and tomatoes with their can juices. Season to taste with salt and pepper.

3 Transfer the vegetable mixture to the slow cooker, stir well, then cover and cook on low for 9 hours until the meat is tender.

4 Remove and discard the bay leaf. Stir in the soured cream and serve immediately.

CARIBBEAN BEEF STEW

Serves: 6

Prep: 20 mins

Cook: 7 hours 40 mins

Ingredients

450 g/1 lb braising steak

450 g/1 lb diced pumpkin or other squash

1 onion, chopped

1 red pepper, deseeded and chopped

2 garlic cloves, finely chopped

2.5-cm/1-inch piece fresh ginger, finely chopped

1 tbsp sweet or hot paprika

225 ml/8 fl oz beef stock

400 g/14 oz canned chopped tomatoes

400 g/14 oz canned pigeon peas or chickpeas, drained and rinsed

400 g/14 oz canned black-eyed beans, drained and rinsed

salt and pepper

Method

1 Trim off any visible fat from the steak, then dice the meat. Heat a large heavy-based saucepan without adding any extra fat. Add the meat and cook, stirring constantly, for a few minutes, until evenly browned.

2 Stir in the pumpkin, onion and red pepper and cook for 1 minute, then add the garlic, ginger and paprika. Pour in the stock and tomatoes and bring to the boil.

3 Transfer the mixture to the slow cooker, cover and cook on low for 7 hours. Add the pigeon peas and black-eyed beans to the stew and season to taste with salt and pepper. Re-cover and cook on high for 30 minutes. Serve immediately.

MEAT DISHES

TRADITIONAL POT ROAST

Serves: 6   **Prep: 20 mins**   **Cook: 9–10 hours**

Ingredients

1 onion, finely chopped

4 carrots, sliced

4 baby turnips, sliced

4 celery sticks, sliced

2 potatoes, sliced

1 sweet potato, sliced

1.3–1.8 kg/3–4 lb topside of beef, in one piece

1 bouquet garni

300 ml/10 fl oz hot beef stock

salt and pepper

Method

1 Place the onion, carrots, turnips, celery, potatoes and sweet potato in the slow cooker and stir to mix well.

2 Rub the beef all over with salt and pepper, then place on top of the bed of vegetables. Add the bouquet garni and pour in the stock. Cover and cook on low for 9–10 hours, until the beef is cooked to your liking. Remove and discard the bouquet garni and serve immediately.

SAUSAGE & BEAN CASSOULET

Serves: 4   **Prep: 20 mins**   **Cook: 6 hours 10 mins**

Ingredients

2 tbsp sunflower oil

2 onions, chopped

2 garlic cloves, finely chopped

115 g/4 oz streaky bacon, chopped

500 g/1 lb 2 oz pork sausages

400 g/14 oz canned haricot, red kidney or black-eyed beans, drained and rinsed

2 tbsp chopped fresh parsley

150 ml/5 fl oz hot beef stock

To serve

4 slices French bread

55 g/2 oz Gruyère cheese, grated

Method

1 Heat the oil in a heavy-based frying pan. Add the onions and cook over a low heat, stirring occasionally, for 5 minutes, until softened. Add the garlic, bacon and sausages and cook, stirring and turning the sausages occasionally, for a further 5 minutes.

2 Using a slotted spoon, transfer the mixture from the frying pan to the slow cooker. Add the beans, parsley and stock, then cover and cook on low for 6 hours.

3 Shortly before serving, preheat the grill. Place the bread slices on the grill rack and lightly toast on one side under the preheated grill. Turn the slices over, sprinkle with the grated cheese and place under the grill until just melted.

4 Serve the cassoulet and the bread slices immediately.

LAMB SHANKS WITH OLIVES

Serves: 4   **Prep: 25 mins**   **Cook: 8 hours 50 mins**

Ingredients

1½ tbsp plain flour

4 lamb shanks

2 tbsp olive oil

1 onion, sliced

2 garlic cloves, finely chopped

2 tsp sweet paprika

400 g/14 oz canned chopped tomatoes

2 tbsp tomato purée

2 carrots, sliced

2 tsp sugar

225 ml/8 fl oz red wine

5-cm/2-inch cinnamon stick

2 fresh rosemary sprigs

115 g/4 oz stoned black olives

2 tbsp lemon juice

2 tbsp chopped fresh mint, plus extra leaves to garnish

salt and pepper

mashed potato, to serve

Method

1 Put the flour into a polythene bag and season well with salt and pepper. Add the lamb and shake well to coat.

2 Heat the oil in a large, heavy-based saucepan. Add the lamb shanks and cook over a medium heat, turning frequently, for 6–8 minutes, until evenly browned. Transfer to a plate.

3 Add the onion and garlic to the saucepan and cook, stirring, for 5 minutes, until softened. Stir in the next 8 ingredients and bring to the boil.

4 Transfer the mixture to the slow cooker and add the lamb shanks. Cover and cook on low for 8 hours, until the lamb is very tender.

5 Add the olives, lemon juice and chopped mint to the slow cooker. Re-cover and cook on high for 30 minutes. Remove and discard the rosemary and cinnamon stick. Serve with mashed potato and garnished with mint leaves.

★ Variation

For a more robust dish, add 400 g/14 oz chickpeas, drained and rinsed, to this Moroccan-inspired dish.

FISH & SEAFOOD DISHES

SALMON CHOWDER

Serves: 4
Prep: 25 mins
Cook: 3 hours 55 mins–4 hours

Ingredients

15 g/½ oz butter

1 tbsp sunflower oil

1 onion, finely chopped

1 leek, finely chopped

1 fennel bulb, finely chopped, feathery tops reserved

280 g/10 oz potatoes, diced

700 ml/1¼ pints fish stock

450 g/1 lb salmon fillet, skinned and cut into cubes

300 ml/10 fl oz milk

150 ml/5 fl oz single cream

2 tbsp chopped fresh dill

salt and pepper

Method

1 Melt the butter with the oil in a saucepan. Add the onion, leek and fennel and cook over a low heat, stirring occasionally, for 5 minutes. Add the potatoes and cook, stirring occasionally, for a further 4 minutes, then pour in the stock and season to taste with salt and pepper. Bring to the boil, then transfer to the slow cooker. Cover and cook on low for 3 hours, until the potatoes are tender.

2 Meanwhile, chop the fennel fronds and set aside. Add the salmon to the slow cooker, pour in the milk and stir gently. Re-cover and cook on low for 30 minutes, until the fish flakes easily.

3 Gently stir in the cream, dill and the reserved fennel fronds, re-cover and cook for a further 10–15 minutes, until heated through. Taste and adjust the seasoning, adding salt and pepper if needed. Serve immediately.

★ Variation

For a deliciously light smoky flavour, replace the fresh salmon fillet with 450 g/1 lb smoked salmon.

FISH & SEAFOOD DISHES

PRAWN BISQUE

Serves: 4–6   **Prep: 25–30 mins**   **Cook: 3 hours 40 mins– 6 hours 40 mins**

Ingredients

1 tbsp butter

1 onion, diced

100 g/3½ oz long-grain rice

2 tbsp tomato purée

1½ tsp salt

½ tsp cayenne pepper

2 litres/3½ pints low-sodium prawn stock or fish stock

1 carrot, diced

1 celery stick, diced

225 g/8 oz mushrooms, diced

675 g/1 lb 8 oz raw prawns, peeled, deveined and cut into bite-sized pieces, if large

150 ml/5 fl oz double cream

2 tbsp lemon juice

snipped chives, to garnish

Method

1 Melt the butter in a large frying pan over a medium–high heat. Add the onion and cook, stirring, for about 5 minutes, until soft. Add the rice, tomato purée, salt and cayenne pepper and cook, stirring, for a further 1 minute. Add a quarter of the stock and cook, stirring, for about 1 minute, scraping up any sediment from the base of the pan.

2 Add the onion mixture to the slow cooker together with the carrot, celery, mushrooms and remaining stock. Cover and cook on high for 3 hours or on low for 6 hours.

3 Using a food processor or blender, purée the soup in batches. Return to the slow cooker, add the prawns, cover and cook on high for 30 minutes, until the prawns are cooked through. Stir in the cream and lemon juice and serve immediately, garnished with the chives.

NEW ENGLAND CLAM CHOWDER

Serves: 4   **Prep: 20 mins**   **Cook: 4 hours 5 mins**

Ingredients

25 g/1 oz butter

1 onion, finely chopped

2 potatoes, peeled and cut into cubes

1 large carrot, diced

400 ml/14 fl oz fish stock or water

280 g/10 oz canned clams, drained

250 ml/9 fl oz double cream

salt and pepper

chopped fresh parsley, to garnish

fresh crusty bread, to serve

Method

1 Melt the butter in a frying pan, add the onion and fry over a medium heat for 4–5 minutes, stirring, until the onion is golden.

2 Transfer the onion to the slow cooker with the potatoes, carrot, stock and salt and pepper to taste. Cover and cook on high for 3 hours.

3 Add the clams and the cream to the slow cooker and stir to mix evenly. Re-cover and cook for a further 1 hour.

4 Serve the chowder immediately, garnished with parsley and served with fresh crusty bread.

GINGER-STEAMED HALIBUT WITH TOMATOES & BEANS

Serves: 4　　　　　**Prep: 25–30 mins,**　　　**Cook: 2 hours**
　　　　　　　　　　　plus marinating

Ingredients

1 tbsp finely chopped
fresh ginger

2 garlic cloves,
finely chopped

1–2 hot red chillies,
deseeded and sliced

2 tbsp Thai fish sauce

2 tbsp mirin or other sweet
white wine

1 tsp sugar

4 halibut fillets (about
675 g/1 lb 8 oz in total)

vegetable oil, for oiling

350 g/12 oz French beans,
topped and tailed

450 g/1 lb cherry tomatoes,
halved, or quartered if large

To garnish

4 spring onions, thinly sliced

fresh coriander, finely
chopped

fresh basil leaves, shredded

Method

1 Put the ginger, garlic, chillies, fish sauce, mirin and sugar into a baking dish large enough to hold the fish and stir to combine. Add the fish and turn to coat in the mixture. Cover and place in the refrigerator to marinate for 30 minutes.

2 Meanwhile, brush four large squares of baking paper with oil.

3 Divide the beans evenly between the prepared squares of paper, piling them in the middle. Scatter the tomatoes evenly over them. Top each pile of vegetables with a fish fillet and some of the marinade. Fold up the packets securely, leaving a little room for the steam to circulate, and place them in the slow cooker. Cover and cook on high for about 2 hours, until the halibut is flaky and cooked through.

4 To serve, carefully remove the packets from the slow cooker, open them and slide the contents onto warmed plates, then garnish with spring onions, coriander and basil.

FISH & SEAFOOD DISHES

POACHED SALMON WITH DILL & LIME

Serves: 4   **Prep: 20 mins**   **Cook: 4 hours 5 mins**

Ingredients

30 g/1 oz butter, melted

1 onion, thinly sliced

450 g/1 lb potatoes, peeled and thinly sliced

100 ml/3½ fl oz hot fish stock or water

4 pieces skinless salmon fillet, about 140 g/5 oz each

juice of 1 lime

2 tbsp chopped fresh dill

salt and pepper

lime wedges, to serve

Method

1 Brush the base of the slow cooker with 1 tablespoon of the butter. Layer the onion and potatoes in the slow cooker, sprinkling with salt and pepper between the layers. Add the stock and dot with 1 tablespoon of the butter. Cover and cook on low for 3 hours.

2 Arrange the salmon over the vegetables in a single layer. Drizzle the lime juice over, sprinkle with dill and salt and pepper to taste and pour the remaining butter on top. Re-cover and cook on low for a further 1 hour, until the fish flakes easily.

3 Serve the salmon and vegetables on warmed plates with the juices spooned over and lime wedges on the side.

SALMON FLORENTINE

Serves: 4   **Prep: 20 mins**   **Cook: 1 hour 40 mins**

Ingredients

150 ml/5 fl oz fish stock

225 ml/8 fl oz dry white wine

2 lemons

1 onion, thinly sliced

4 salmon fillets, about 175 g/6 oz each

1 bouquet garni

1.3 kg/3 lb spinach, coarse stalks removed

freshly grated nutmeg, to taste

175 g/6 oz unsalted butter, plus extra for greasing

salt and pepper

Method

1 Lightly grease the slow cooker base with butter. Pour the stock and wine into a saucepan and bring to the boil. Meanwhile, thinly slice one of the lemons. Put half the lemon slices and all the onion slices over the base of the slow cooker pot and top with the salmon fillets. Season to taste with salt and pepper, add the bouquet garni and cover the fish with the remaining lemon slices. Pour the hot stock mixture over the fish, cover and cook on low for 1½ hours, until the fish flakes easily.

2 Meanwhile, finely grate the rind and squeeze the juice from the remaining lemon. When the fish is nearly ready, cook the spinach, in just the water clinging to the leaves after washing, for 3–5 minutes, until wilted. Drain well, squeezing out as much water as possible. Chop finely, arrange on a warmed serving dish and season to taste with salt, pepper and nutmeg.

3 Carefully lift the fish out of the slow cooker and discard the lemon slices, onion slices and bouquet garni. Put the salmon fillets on the bed of spinach and keep warm.

4 Melt the butter in a saucepan over a low heat. Stir in the lemon rind and half the juice. Pour the lemon butter sauce over the fish and serve.

FISH & SEAFOOD DISHES

PASTA & PRAWNS

Serves: 4   **Prep: 15 mins**   **Cook: 7¼ hours**

Ingredients

400 g/14 oz tomatoes, peeled and chopped

140 g/5 oz tomato purée

1 garlic clove, finely chopped

2 tbsp chopped fresh parsley

500 g/1 lb 2 oz cooked, peeled Mediterranean prawns

6 fresh basil leaves, torn

400 g/14 oz dried tagliatelle

salt and pepper

fresh basil leaves, to garnish

Method

1 Put the tomatoes, tomato purée, garlic and parsley in the slow cooker and season with salt and pepper. Cover and cook on low for 7 hours.

2 Add the prawns and basil. Re-cover and cook on high for 15 minutes.

3 Meanwhile, bring a large saucepan of lightly salted water to the boil. Add the pasta, bring back to the boil and cook for 10–12 minutes until tender but still firm to the bite.

4 Drain the pasta and tip it into a warmed serving bowl. Add the prawn sauce and toss lightly with 2 large forks. Garnish with the basil leaves and serve immediately.

FISH & SEAFOOD DISHES

SALMON WITH LEEKS & CREAM

Serves: 4   **Prep: 20–25 mins**   **Cook: 2¼ hours**

Ingredients

vegetable oil, for oiling

2 tbsp butter

2 leeks, white and light green parts halved lengthways, then thinly sliced crossways

50 ml/2 fl oz dry white wine

125 ml/4 fl oz double cream

1 tsp salt

½ tsp pepper

4 salmon fillets, about 175 g/6 oz each

8 small fresh sage leaves

Method

1 Lightly brush four large squares of baking paper with oil.

2 Heat the butter in a large frying pan over a medium–high heat, until melted and bubbling. Add the leeks and cook, stirring occasionally, for about 5 minutes, until soft.

3 Stir in the wine and bring to the boil. Cook, stirring and scraping up any sediment from the base of the pan, for a further 3 minutes, or until most of the wine has evaporated. Stir in the cream, salt and pepper and cook, stirring, for about 2 minutes, until the cream is beginning to thicken.

4 Place one salmon fillet in the centre of each prepared paper square. Top with the leek and cream mixture, then place two sage leaves on top of each portion. Fold up the packets securely, leaving a little room for the steam to circulate, then place them in the slow cooker. Cover and cook on high for about 2 hours, until the salmon is cooked through.

5 To serve, carefully remove the packets from the slow cooker, open them and slide the contents onto warmed plates. Serve immediately.

FISH & SEAFOOD DISHES

TAGLIATELLE WITH TUNA

Serves: 4

Prep: 20 mins

Cook: 2 hours 10 mins

Ingredients

200 g/7 oz dried egg tagliatelle

400 g/14 oz canned tuna steak in oil, drained

1 bunch spring onions, sliced

175 g/6 oz frozen peas

2 tsp hot chilli sauce

600 ml/1 pint hot chicken stock

115 g/4 oz grated Cheddar cheese

salt and pepper

Method

1 Bring a large saucepan of lightly salted water to the boil. Add the pasta, return to the boil and cook for 2 minutes, until the pasta ribbons are loose. Drain.

2 Break up the tuna into bite-sized chunks and place in the slow cooker with the pasta, spring onions and peas. Season to taste with salt and pepper.

3 Add the chilli sauce to the stock and pour over the ingredients in the slow cooker. Sprinkle the grated cheese over the top. Cover and cook on low for 2 hours. Serve immediately on warmed plates.

SEA BREAM IN LEMON SAUCE

Serves: 4　　　　**Prep: 15 mins**　　　　**Cook: 1¾ hours**

Ingredients

8 sea bream fillets

55 g/2 oz unsalted butter

25 g/1 oz plain flour

850 ml/1½ pints warm milk

4 tbsp lemon juice

225 g/8 oz mushrooms, sliced

1 bouquet garni

salt and pepper

lemon wedges and griddled asparagus, to serve

Method

1　Put the fish fillets into the slow cooker and set aside.

2　Melt the butter in a saucepan over a low heat. Add the flour and cook, stirring constantly, for 1 minute. Gradually stir in the milk, a little at a time, and bring to the boil, stirring constantly. Stir in the lemon juice and mushrooms, add the bouquet garni and season to taste with salt and pepper. Reduce the heat and simmer for 5 minutes. Pour the sauce over the fish fillets, cover and cook on low for 1½ hours.

3　Carefully lift out the fish fillets and transfer to warmed serving plates. Serve immediately with lemon wedges and griddled asparagus.

RED SNAPPER WITH FENNEL

Serves: 4   **Prep: 20 mins**   **Cook: 1½–1¾ hours**

Ingredients

4 whole red snapper, about
350 g/12 oz each, cleaned

1 orange, halved and
thinly sliced

2 garlic cloves, thinly sliced

6 fresh thyme sprigs

1 tbsp olive oil

1 fennel bulb, thinly sliced

450 ml/16 fl oz orange juice

1 bay leaf

1 tsp dill seeds

salt and pepper

salad leaves, to serve

Method

1 Season the fish inside and outside with salt
and pepper. Make 3–4 diagonal slashes on
each side. Divide the orange slices between the
cavities and add 2–3 garlic slices and a thyme
sprig to each. Put the remaining garlic and
thyme in the slashes.

2 Heat the oil in a large frying pan. Add the fennel
and cook over a medium heat, stirring frequently,
for 3–5 minutes, until just softened. Add the
orange juice and bay leaf, and bring to the boil,
then reduce the heat and simmer for a further
5 minutes.

3 Transfer the fennel mixture to the slow cooker. Put
the fish on top and sprinkle with the dill seeds.
Cover and cook on high for 1¼–1½ hours, until
the flesh flakes easily.

4 Carefully transfer the fish to warmed individual
plates. Remove and discard the bay leaf. Spoon
the fennel and some of the cooking juices over
the fish and serve immediately with salad leaves.

POLLOCK BAKE

Serves: 4 **Prep: 15 mins** **Cook: 2 hours 5 mins**

Ingredients

1 tbsp olive oil

1 red onion, sliced

1 yellow pepper, deseeded and sliced

4 pollock fillets, about 140 g/5 oz each

2 tomatoes, thinly sliced

8 stoned black olives, halved

1 garlic clove, thinly sliced

2 tsp balsamic vinegar

juice of 1 orange

salt and pepper

Method

1 Heat the oil in a frying pan, add the onion and yellow pepper and fry over a high heat for 3–4 minutes, stirring, until lightly browned. Transfer to the slow cooker, cover and cook on high for 1 hour.

2 Arrange the fish fillets over the vegetables and season to taste with salt and pepper. Arrange a layer of tomatoes and olives over the top and sprinkle with the garlic and vinegar. Pour over the orange juice, cover and cook on high for a further 1 hour. Serve immediately.

FISH & SEAFOOD DISHES

FRENCH-STYLE FISH STEW

Serves: 4–6 **Prep: 30 mins,** plus chilling **Cook: 6¾ hours**

Ingredients

large pinch of saffron

1 prepared squid

900 g/2 lb mixed white fish, filleted and cut into large chunks

24 large raw prawns, peeled and deveined, heads and shells reserved

2 tbsp olive oil

1 onion, finely chopped

1 fennel bulb, thinly sliced

2 large garlic cloves

4 tbsp Pernod

1 litre/1¾ pints fish stock

400 g/14 oz canned chopped tomatoes

1 tbsp tomato purée

pinch of sugar

salt and pepper

Method

1 Toast the saffron in a dry frying pan over a high heat for 1 minute. Set aside. Cut off and reserve the tentacles from the squid and slice the body into 5-mm/¼-inch rings. Place the seafood and fish in a bowl, cover and chill in the refrigerator until required. Tie the heads and shells of the prawns in a piece of muslin.

2 Heat the oil in a frying pan. Add the onion and fennel and cook over a low heat, for 5 minutes. Crush and add the garlic and cook for 2 minutes. Remove the pan from the heat. Heat the Pernod in a saucepan, ignite and pour it over the onion and fennel, gently shaking the frying pan until the flames have died down.

3 Return the frying pan to the heat, stir in the toasted saffron, stock, tomatoes, tomato purée and sugar, and season to taste with salt and pepper. Bring to the boil, then transfer to the slow cooker, add the bag of prawn shells, cover and cook on low for 6 hours.

4 Remove and discard the bag of prawn shells. Add the fish and seafood to the slow cooker, cover and cook on high for 30 minutes until the fish flakes easily. Serve immediately.

FISH & SEAFOOD DISHES

HALIBUT WITH FENNEL & OLIVES

Serves: 4　　　　**Prep: 30 mins**　　　　**Cook: 2 hours**

Ingredients

vegetable oil, for brushing

2 tbsp olive oil

50 g/1¾ oz stoned
Kalamata olives, chopped

1 garlic clove,
finely chopped

1 small shallot,
finely chopped

zest of 1 lemon

1 tbsp finely chopped
fresh oregano

1 fennel bulb, thinly sliced

4 halibut fillets,
about 175 g/6 oz each

50 ml/2 fl oz dry white wine

cooked couscous, to serve

Method

1　Lightly brush four 30 x 30-cm/12 x 12-inch squares of baking paper with vegetable oil.

2　Put the olive oil, olives, garlic, shallot, lemon zest and oregano into a bowl and mix to combine.

3　Pile equal amounts of the fennel slices in the middle of the prepared squares of baking paper. Top each pile of fennel with a halibut fillet. Spoon the olive mixture over the fish.

4　Drizzle the wine over the fish. Fold up the packets, leaving a little room for the steam to circulate and place them in the slow cooker. Cover and cook on high for about 2 hours, until the fish is cooked through.

5　To serve, open up the packets and gently transfer the contents to warmed plates. Serve immediately with couscous.

FISH & SEAFOOD DISHES

MOROCCAN SEA BREAM

Serves: 2　　　**Prep: 20 mins**　　　**Cook: 6¾–7 hours**

Ingredients

2 tbsp olive oil

2 onions, chopped

2 garlic cloves, finely chopped

2 carrots, finely chopped

1 fennel bulb, finely chopped

½ tsp ground cumin

½ tsp ground cloves

1 tsp ground coriander

pinch of saffron threads

300 ml/10 fl oz fish stock

1 preserved or fresh lemon

900 g/2 lb sea bream, cleaned

salt and pepper

Method

1 Heat the oil in a large, heavy-based saucepan. Add the onions, garlic, carrots and fennel and cook over a medium heat, stirring occasionally, for 5 minutes. Stir in all the spices and cook, stirring, for a further 2 minutes. Pour in the stock, season to taste with salt and pepper and bring to the boil.

2 Transfer the mixture to the slow cooker. Cover and cook on low for 6 hours or until the vegetables are tender.

3 Rinse the preserved lemon if using. Discard the fish head if you like. Slice the lemon and place the slices in the fish cavity, then place the fish in the slow cooker. Re-cover and cook on high for 30–45 minutes until the flesh flakes easily.

4 Carefully transfer the fish to a platter and spoon the vegetables around it. Cover and keep warm. Transfer the cooking liquid to a saucepan and boil for a few minutes until reduced. Spoon it over the fish and serve immediately.

FISH & SEAFOOD DISHES

MIXED MEDITERRANEAN SHELLFISH

Serves: 8 **Prep: 30 mins** **Cook: 7 hours 50 mins**

Ingredients

1 tbsp olive oil

115 g/4 oz bacon, diced

2 tbsp butter

2 shallots, chopped

2 leeks, sliced

2 celery sticks, chopped

2 potatoes, diced

675 g/1 lb 8 oz tomatoes, peeled, deseeded and chopped

3 tbsp chopped fresh parsley

3 tbsp snipped fresh chives, plus extra to garnish

1 bay leaf

1 fresh thyme sprig

1.4 litres/2½ pints fish stock

24 live mussels

24 live clams

450 g/1 lb sea bream fillets

24 raw tiger prawns

salt and pepper

Method

1 Heat the oil in a heavy-based frying pan. Add the bacon and cook, stirring frequently, for 5–8 minutes until crisp. Using a slotted spoon, transfer to the slow cooker. Add the butter to the frying pan and when it has melted, add the shallots, leeks, celery and potatoes. Cook over a low heat, stirring occasionally, for 5 minutes until softened. Stir in the tomatoes, parsley, chives, bay leaf and thyme, pour in the stock and bring to the boil, stirring constantly. Pour the mixture into the slow cooker, cover and cook on low for 7 hours.

2 Meanwhile, scrub the mussels and clams under cold running water and pull off the 'beards' from the mussels. Discard any with broken shells or that do not shut immediately when sharply tapped. Cut the fish fillets into bite-sized chunks. Peel and devein the prawns.

3 Remove and discard the bay leaf and thyme sprig from the stew. Season to taste with salt and pepper and add all the fish and seafood. Re-cover and cook on high for 30 minutes. Discard any shellfish that remain closed. Serve immediately garnished with extra chives.

JAMBALAYA

Serves: 4   **Prep: 25 mins**   **Cook: 6¾ hours**

Ingredients

½ tsp cayenne pepper

½ tsp pepper

1 tsp salt

2 tsp chopped fresh thyme

350 g/12 oz skinless, boneless chicken breasts, diced

2 tbsp corn oil

2 onions, chopped

2 garlic cloves, finely chopped

2 green peppers, deseeded and chopped

2 celery sticks, chopped

115 g/4 oz smoked ham, chopped

175 g/6 oz chorizo sausage, sliced

400 g/14 oz canned chopped tomatoes

2 tbsp tomato purée

225 ml/8 fl oz chicken stock

450 g/1 lb raw prawns, peeled and deveined

450 g/1 lb cooked rice

salt and pepper

snipped fresh chives, to garnish

Method

1 Mix together the cayenne pepper, pepper, salt and thyme in a bowl. Add the chicken and toss to coat.

2 Heat the oil in a large, heavy-based saucepan. Add the onions, garlic, green peppers and celery and cook over a low heat, stirring occasionally, for 5 minutes. Add the chicken and cook over a medium heat, stirring frequently, for a further 5 minutes, until golden all over. Stir in the ham, chorizo, tomatoes, tomato purée and stock and bring to the boil.

3 Transfer the mixture to the slow cooker. Cover and cook on low for 6 hours. Add the prawns and rice, re-cover and cook on high for 30 minutes.

4 Taste and adjust the seasoning, adding salt and pepper if necessary. Transfer to warmed plates, garnish with chives and serve immediately.

LOUISIANA GUMBO

Serves: 6   **Prep: 25–30 mins**   **Cook: 5 hours 50 mins–6 hours 50 mins**

Ingredients

2 tbsp sunflower oil

175 g/6 oz okra, cut into 2.5-cm/1-inch pieces

2 onions, finely chopped

4 celery sticks, very finely chopped

1 garlic clove, finely chopped

2 tbsp plain flour

½ tsp sugar

1 tsp ground cumin

700 ml/1¼ pints fish stock

1 each red and green pepper, deseeded and chopped

2 large tomatoes, chopped

4 tbsp chopped fresh parsley

1 tbsp chopped fresh coriander

hot pepper sauce

350 g/12 oz large raw prawns, peeled and deveined

350 g/12 oz cod or haddock fillets, skinned and cut into 2.5-cm/1-inch chunks

350 g/12 oz monkfish fillet, cut into 2.5-cm/1-inch chunks

salt and pepper

Method

1 Heat half the oil in a heavy-based frying pan. Add the okra and cook over a low heat, stirring frequently, for 5 minutes until browned. Using a slotted spoon, transfer the okra to the slow cooker.

2 Add the remaining oil to the pan. Add the onions and celery and cook over a low heat, stirring occasionally, for 5 minutes until softened. Add the garlic and cook, stirring frequently, for 1 minute, then sprinkle in the flour, sugar and cumin, and season to taste with salt and pepper. Cook, stirring constantly, for 2 minutes, then remove the pan from the heat.

3 Gradually stir in the stock, then return the pan to the heat and bring to the boil, stirring constantly. Pour the mixture over the okra and stir in the peppers and tomatoes. Cover and cook on low for 5–6 hours.

4 Stir in the parsley, coriander and hot pepper sauce to taste, then add the prawns, cod and monkfish. Cover and cook on high for 30 minutes, until the fish is cooked and the prawns have changed colour. Taste and adjust the seasoning if necessary and serve immediately.

FISH & SEAFOOD DISHES

EASY BOUILLABAISSE

Serves: 4 **Prep: 30 mins** **Cook: 2½–4½ hours**

Ingredients

pinch of saffron threads

1 tbsp hot water

2 tbsp olive oil

1 onion, diced

3 garlic cloves, finely chopped

2 celery sticks, finely chopped

1 tsp salt

¼–½ tsp dried red pepper flakes

350 ml/12 fl oz dry white wine

400 g/14 oz canned tomato purée

400 g/14 oz canned chopped tomatoes, with juice

12 small live clams, scrubbed

12 live mussels, scrubbed and debearded

450 g/1 lb white fish fillet, cut into 5-cm/2-inch pieces

225 g/8 oz raw prawns, peeled and deveined

2 tbsp finely chopped fresh parsley, to garnish

aïoli, to serve

Method

1 Place the saffron in a small bowl and cover with the hot water. Heat the oil in a large frying pan over a medium–high heat. Add the onion and garlic and cook, stirring, for about 5 minutes, until soft. Add the celery, salt and red pepper flakes, then add the wine. Bring to the boil and cook, stirring, for about 8 minutes, until the liquid is reduced by half. Transfer the mixture to the slow cooker.

2 Stir in the saffron and its soaking water, tomato purée and tomatoes with their can juices. Cover and cook on high for about 2 hours or on low for about 4 hours.

3 Discard any clams or mussels with broken shells and any that refuse to close when tapped. Add the fish, prawns, clams and mussels, re-cover and cook on high for a further 10–15 minutes, until the fish and prawns are cooked through and the clams and mussels have opened, discarding any that still remain closed.

4 To serve, ladle some broth into four serving bowls, then add some of the fish and shellfish. Top each serving with a dollop of aïoli, garnish with parsley and serve immediately.

SOLE & PRAWN CREAM

Serves: 4 **Prep: 30 mins** **Cook: 2 hours 50 mins–
2 hours 55 mins**

Ingredients

900 g/2 lb potatoes,
cut into chunks

700 g/1 lb 9 oz sole fillets

25 g/1 oz butter,
plus extra for greasing

2 egg yolks

175 g/6 oz Cheddar
cheese, grated

1 tbsp chopped fresh
flat-leaf parsley, plus extra
sprigs to garnish

550 g/1 lb 4 oz cooked
peeled prawns

salt and pepper

Method

1 Cook the potatoes in a saucepan of lightly
salted boiling water for 20–25 minutes.

2 Meanwhile, grease a 1.2-litre/2-pint pudding
basin with butter, then line it with the fish
fillets, skin-side inwards and with the tail ends
overlapping the rim. Cut out a double round
of greaseproof paper that is 5 cm/2 inches
wider than the rim of the basin. Grease one
side with butter.

3 Drain the potatoes and return to the saucepan
with the butter. Remove from the heat, mash
well and stir in the egg yolks, cheese and parsley.
Season lightly with salt and pepper.

4 Make alternating layers of the potato mixture
and prawns in the basin, then fold over the fish
fillets. Cover with the greaseproof paper and tie
in place with string.

5 Stand the basin on a trivet in the slow cooker
and pour in water to come halfway up the side.
Cover and cook on low for 2½ hours.

6 Remove the basin from the slow cooker,
discarding the greaseproof paper. Turn out
onto a serving dish. Serve garnished with
parsley sprigs.

FISH & SEAFOOD DISHES

SEAFOOD IN SAFFRON SAUCE

Serves: 4　　　　**Prep: 20 mins**　　　　**Cook: 5¾ hours**

Ingredients

2 tbsp olive oil

1 onion, sliced

pinch of saffron threads

1 tbsp chopped
fresh thyme

2 garlic cloves,
finely chopped

800 g/1 lb 12 oz canned
chopped tomatoes

175 ml/6 fl oz dry white wine

2 litres/3½ pints fish stock

225 g/8 oz live clams

225 g/8 oz live mussels

350 g/12 oz red mullet fillets

450 g/1 lb monkfish fillets

225 g/8 oz squid rings,
thawed if frozen

2 tbsp shredded fresh basil

salt and pepper

Method

1　Heat the oil in a heavy-based frying pan. Add the onion, saffron, thyme and a pinch of salt, and cook over a low heat, stirring occasionally, for 5 minutes until softened. Add the garlic and cook, stirring constantly, for 2 minutes.

2　Drain and add the tomatoes, wine and stock, season to taste with salt and pepper, and bring to the boil, stirring constantly. Transfer the mixture to the slow cooker, cover and cook on low for 5 hours.

3　Meanwhile, scrub the shellfish under cold running water and pull the 'beards' off the mussels. Discard any with broken shells or that do not shut immediately when sharply tapped. Cut the mullet and monkfish fillets into bite-sized chunks.

4　Add the pieces of fish, the shellfish and the squid rings to the slow cooker, re-cover and cook on high for 30 minutes, until the clams and mussels have opened and the fish is cooked through. Discard any shellfish that remain closed. Stir in the basil and serve immediately.

FISH & SEAFOOD DISHES

CLAMS IN SPICY BROTH WITH CHORIZO

Serves: 4 **Prep: 25 mins** **Cook: 2 hours 25 mins–
4 hours 25 mins**

Ingredients

1 tbsp olive oil

1 red onion, halved
lengthways and sliced

115 g/4 oz chorizo
sausage, diced

1 fennel bulb,
coarsely chopped

400 g/14 oz canned
chopped tomatoes

125 ml/4 fl oz dry white wine

125 ml/4 fl oz clam
juice or water

½ tsp salt

¼–½ tsp crushed
red pepper flakes

900 g/2 lb small live clams,
scrubbed

2 tbsp chopped fresh
flat-leaf parsley, to garnish

Method

1 Heat the oil in a large frying pan over a medium–
   high heat. Add the onion and cook, stirring, for
   about 5 minutes, until soft. Add the chorizo and
   continue to cook, stirring occasionally, until the
   meat begins to brown. Transfer the mixture to the
   slow cooker.

2 Stir in the fennel, tomatoes and their can juices,
   wine, clam juice, salt and red pepper flakes.
   Cover and cook on high for about 2 hours or on
   low for about 4 hours.

3 Discard any clams with broken shells and
   any that refuse to close when tapped. Add
   the clams to the slow cooker, re-cover and cook
   on high for a further 10–15 minutes, until the
   clams have opened. Discard any clams that
   remain closed.

4 Serve the clams in bowls, with a generous
   amount of broth and garnished with parsley.

SOUTH-WESTERN SEAFOOD STEW

Serves: 4   **Prep: 25 mins**   **Cook: 8¼ hours**

Ingredients

2 tbsp olive oil, plus extra for drizzling

1 large onion, chopped

4 garlic cloves, finely chopped

1 yellow pepper, deseeded and chopped

1 red pepper, deseeded and chopped

1 orange pepper, deseeded and chopped

450 g/1 lb tomatoes, peeled and chopped

2 large mild green chillies, such as poblano, chopped

finely grated rind and juice of 1 lime

2 tbsp chopped fresh coriander, plus extra leaves to garnish

1 bay leaf

450 ml/16 fl oz fish, vegetable or chicken stock

450 g/1 lb red mullet fillets

450 g/1 lb raw prawns

225 g/8 oz prepared squid

salt and pepper

Method

1 Heat the oil in a saucepan. Add the onion and garlic and cook over a low heat, stirring occasionally, for 5 minutes, until softened. Add the peppers, tomatoes and chillies and cook, stirring frequently, for 5 minutes. Stir in the lime rind and juice, add the chopped coriander and bay leaf and pour in the stock. Bring to the boil, stirring occasionally.

2 Transfer the mixture to the slow cooker, cover and cook on low for 7½ hours. Meanwhile, skin the fish fillets, if necessary, and cut the flesh into chunks. Peel and devein the prawns. Cut the squid bodies into rings and halve the tentacles or leave them whole.

3 Add the seafood to the stew, season to taste with salt and pepper, re-cover and cook on high for 30 minutes, or until tender and cooked through. Remove and discard the bay leaf. Transfer to warmed serving bowls, garnish with coriander leaves and serve immediately.

★ **Variation**

For a spicier version of this stew, use a hotter variety of fresh chilli and add ½ teaspoon chilli powder and ½ teaspoon of cumin, or to taste.

MEAT-FREE MEALS

GREEK BEAN & VEGETABLE SOUP

Serves: 4–6

Prep: 25 mins, plus soaking

Cook: 12 hours 20 mins

Ingredients

500g/1 lb 2 oz dried haricot beans, soaked in cold water overnight

2 onions, finely chopped

2 garlic cloves, finely chopped

2 potatoes, chopped

2 carrots, chopped

2 tomatoes, peeled and chopped

2 celery sticks, chopped

4 tbsp extra virgin olive oil

1 bay leaf

salt and pepper

12 black olives, pitted and sliced and 2 tbsp snipped chives, to garnish

Method

1 Drain the beans and rinse well under cold running water. Place the beans in a saucepan, cover with fresh cold water and bring to the boil. Boil rapidly for at least 10 minutes, then remove from the heat, drain and rinse again.

2 Place the beans in the slow cooker and add the onions, garlic, potatoes, carrots, tomatoes, celery, olive oil and bay leaf.

3 Pour in 2 litres/3½ pints of boiling water, making sure that all the ingredients are fully submerged. Cover and cook on low for 12 hours until the beans are tender.

4 Remove and discard the bay leaf. Season the soup to taste with salt and pepper and garnish with the olives and chives. Transfer into warmed soup bowls and serve immediately.

★ Variation

You can vary the beans used in this soup and also the vegetables depending on what is in season.

ITALIAN BREAD SOUP WITH GREENS

Serves: 4   **Prep: 20 mins**   **Cook: 4 hours 35 mins–8 hours 35 mins**

Ingredients

2 tbsp olive oil

1 onion, diced

1 leek, halved lengthways and thinly sliced

2 litres/3½ pints vegetable stock

200 g/7 oz kale, chopped

2 celery sticks, diced

2 carrots, diced

1 tsp crumbled dried oregano

1½ tsp salt

½ tsp pepper

200 g/7 oz day-old cubed sourdough bread

30 g/1 oz freshly grated Parmesan cheese, to garnish

Method

1 Heat the oil in a large frying pan over a medium–high heat. Add the onion and leek and sauté for about 5 minutes, until soft.

2 Transfer the mixture to the slow cooker and add the stock, kale, celery, carrots, oregano, salt and pepper. Cover and cook on high for about 4 hours or on low for 8 hours.

3 Add the bread to the soup, re-cover and cook on high, stirring occasionally, for about 30 minutes, until the bread breaks down and thickens the soup.

4 Serve immediately, garnished with the cheese.

CARROT & CORIANDER SOUP

Serves: 6   **Prep: 20–25 mins**   **Cook: 4 hours 40 mins–5 hours 40 mins**

Ingredients

1 tbsp butter

1½ tbsp sunflower oil

1 Spanish onion, finely chopped

500 g/1 lb 2 oz carrots, diced

1-cm/½-inch piece fresh ginger

2 tsp ground coriander

1 tsp plain flour

1.2 litres/2 pints vegetable stock

150 ml/5 fl oz soured cream

2 tbsp chopped fresh coriander

salt and pepper

Method

1 Melt the butter with the oil in a saucepan. Add the onion, carrots and ginger, cover and cook over a low heat, stirring occasionally, for 8 minutes, until softened and just beginning to colour.

2 Sprinkle over the ground coriander and flour and cook, stirring constantly, for 1 minute. Gradually stir in the stock, a little at a time, and bring to the boil, stirring constantly. Season to taste with salt and pepper.

3 Transfer the mixture to the slow cooker, cover and cook on low for 4–5 hours. Ladle the soup into a food processor or blender, in batches if necessary, and process until smooth. Return the soup to the slow cooker and stir in the soured cream. Cover and cook on low for a further 15–20 minutes, until heated through.

4 Ladle the soup into warmed bowls and garnish with the chopped coriander. Serve immediately.

MEAT-FREE MEALS

PEARS STUFFED WITH BLUE CHEESE

Serves: 4   **Prep: 20 mins**   **Cook: 2 hours,**
plus 1–2 mins optional grilling

Ingredients

2 just-ripe pears

115 g/4 oz Gorgonzola
cheese or other blue
cheese

1 tbsp honey

30 g/1 oz pecan nuts or
walnuts, chopped

Method

1 Fill the slow cooker with water to a depth of about 2.5 cm/1 inch.

2 Halve the pears lengthways and scoop out the core. Slice off a bit from the outside of each pear half to make a flat surface so that the pears will sit level when placed in the slow cooker.

3 Divide the cheese equally between the pears, pressing it into the hollows. Place the pears cheese side up in the slow cooker in a single layer and drizzle the honey evenly over them. Cover and cook on high for about 2 hours, until soft.

4 Remove the pears from the slow cooker with a slotted spoon. Arrange on a serving plate and sprinkle the nuts evenly over each half. If liked, brown the pears under the grill for 1-2 minutes. Serve immediately.

TUSCAN WHITE BEAN SPREAD WITH ROASTED GARLIC

Serves: 6-8

Prep: 20 mins, plus cooling

Cook: 6 hours

Ingredients

1 garlic bulb

3 tbsp olive oil

400 g/14 oz canned cannellini beans, rinsed and drained

2 tbsp lemon juice

2 tsp finely chopped fresh rosemary

1/8–1/4 tsp cayenne pepper, plus extra to taste

85 g/3 oz freshly grated Parmesan cheese

salt

baguette slices, to serve

Method

1 Keeping the garlic bulb intact, slice about 1 cm/½ inch off the top, exposing the cloves. Fill the slow cooker with water to a depth of about 5 mm/¼ inch. Stand the garlic bulb cut side up in the slow cooker and drizzle 1 tablespoon of the oil over the top. Cover and cook on low for about 6 hours, until the garlic is soft and golden brown. Remove the garlic, leave to cool, then squeeze the cloves into a small bowl.

2 Put the beans, half of the roasted garlic (reserve the remaining garlic for another recipe), lemon juice, rosemary, cayenne pepper and ¼ teaspoon of salt into a food processor and process until smooth.

3 Add the cheese and pulse until well combined. If the mixture is too thick, add a further 1-2 tablespoons of the oil and pulse to incorporate. Taste and add more salt and cayenne pepper if necessary. Serve with baguette slices.

INDIAN-SPICED CHICKPEAS

Serves: 4   **Prep: 20 mins**   **Cook: 6 hours 10 mins**

Ingredients

2 tbsp vegetable oil

1 onion, finely chopped

2 garlic cloves, finely chopped

1 tsp ground cumin

1 tsp ground turmeric

1 tsp ground ginger

¼–½ tsp cayenne pepper

350 ml/12 fl oz water

800 g/1 lb 12 oz canned chickpeas, rinsed and drained

1 tsp salt

½ tsp garam masala

To serve

steamed rice

yogurt and cucumber salad

Method

1 Heat the oil in a large frying pan over a medium-high heat. Add the onion and garlic and cook, stirring, for about 5 minutes, until soft. Add the cumin, turmeric, ginger and cayenne pepper and cook, stirring, for a further 1 minute. Add the water and cook for a further 1–2 minutes, scraping up any sediment from the base of the pan. Transfer the mixture to the slow cooker.

2 Stir in the chickpeas, cover and cook on low for about 6 hours.

3 Just before serving, add the salt and garam masala. Serve immediately with rice, and a yogurt and cucumber salad.

MEAT-FREE MEALS

VEGETABLE PASTA

Serves: 4　　　　**Prep: 20 mins**　　　　**Cook: 3 hours 25 mins**

Ingredients

250 g/9 oz dried penne pasta

2 tbsp olive oil, plus extra for drizzling

1 red onion, sliced

2 courgettes, thinly sliced

200 g/7 oz closed cup mushrooms, sliced

2 tbsp chopped fresh oregano

300 g/10½ oz tomatoes, sliced

55 g/2 oz freshly grated Parmesan cheese

salt and pepper

Method

1 Bring a large pan of lightly salted water to the boil. Add the pasta, bring back to the boil and cook for 8–10 minutes, or until tender but still firm to the bite. Drain. Meanwhile, heat the oil in a heavy-based saucepan, add the onion and cook over a medium heat, stirring occasionally, for 5 minutes, until softened. Stir into the pasta.

2 Place a layer of courgettes and mushrooms in the slow cooker and top with a layer of pasta. Sprinkle with oregano, salt and pepper and continue layering, finishing with a layer of vegetables.

3 Arrange the sliced tomatoes on top and drizzle with oil. Cover and cook on high for 3 hours, or until tender.

4 Sprinkle with cheese, re-cover and cook for a further 10 minutes. Transfer to a warmed serving bowl and serve immediately.

MEAT-FREE MEALS

LOUISIANA COURGETTES

Serves: 6 **Prep: 20 mins** **Cook: 2½ hours**

Ingredients

1 kg/2 lb 4 oz courgettes, thickly sliced

1 onion, finely chopped

2 garlic cloves, finely chopped

2 red peppers, deseeded and chopped

5 tbsp hot vegetable stock

4 tomatoes, peeled and chopped

25 g/1 oz butter, diced

salt and cayenne pepper

crusty bread, to serve

Method

1 Place the courgettes, onion, garlic and red peppers in the slow cooker and season to taste with salt and cayenne pepper. Pour in the stock and mix well.

2 Sprinkle the chopped tomatoes on top and dot with the butter. Cover and cook on high for 2½ hours until tender. Serve immediately with crusty bread.

STUFFED PEPPERS

Serves: 4   **Prep: 20 mins**   **Cook: 5 hours 10 mins**

Ingredients

100 g/3½ oz basmati rice

4 red peppers

400 g/14 oz canned chickpeas, drained

100 g/3½ oz canned or frozen sweetcorn

4 spring onions, sliced

1 tbsp chopped fresh thyme

1 tbsp olive oil

150 ml/5 fl oz vegetable stock

salt and pepper

Method

1 Cook the rice in lightly salted, boiling water for 10 minutes, until almost tender. Drain well.

2 Slice the tops from the peppers and remove the seeds and membranes. Cut a small slice from the base of each so they sit firmly.

3 Mix the rice, chickpeas, sweetcorn, onions, thyme, oil and salt and pepper together. Spoon into the peppers and replace the lids.

4 Place the peppers in the slow cooker. Pour in the stock, cover and cook on low for 5 hours, until tender. Transfer to warmed serving plates and serve immediately.

BAKED EGGS WITH CARAMELIZED ONIONS & CHEESE

Serves: 4　　　　**Prep: 25 mins**　　　　**Cook: 1¼ hours**

Ingredients

4 tbsp butter, plus extra for greasing

1 onion, halved and thinly sliced

4 tbsp double cream

55 g/2 oz freshly grated Parmesan cheese

4 large eggs

8 small fresh sage leaves

salt and pepper

Method

1 Grease four 175-g/6-oz ramekins with butter. Fill the slow cooker with hot water to a depth of 2.5 cm/1 inch, cover and turn on to high.

2 Melt the butter in a large frying pan over a medium–high heat. Add the onion and cook, stirring occasionally, for about 6 minutes, until soft and just beginning to brown. Reduce the heat to medium, add 3 tablespoons of the cream and continue to cook, stirring occasionally, for a further 5 minutes, or until the cream is beginning to thicken.

3 Stir in the cheese. Season the mixture to taste with salt and pepper and divide between the prepared ramekins.

4 Break an egg into each ramekin, season with a little more salt and pepper, then top each egg with two sage leaves and evenly drizzle the remaining cream over the eggs.

5 Cover each ramekin with foil and place carefully in the water bath in the slow cooker. Cover the slow cooker and cook on high for about 1 hour, until the eggs are set to your liking. Serve immediately in the ramekins.

MEAT-FREE MEALS

MACARONI CHEESE WITH TOASTED BREADCRUMBS

Serves: 4   **Prep: 20 mins**   **Cook: 2 hours 20 mins–4 hours 20 mins**

Ingredients

vegetable oil, for brushing

2 tbsp butter

2 tbsp plain flour

150 ml/5 fl oz vegetable stock

450 ml/16 fl oz evaporated milk

1½ tsp mustard powder

⅛–¼ tsp cayenne pepper

1 tsp salt

175 g/6 oz Gruyère cheese, grated

175 g/6 oz fontina cheese, grated

55 g/2 oz freshly grated Parmesan cheese

350 g/12 oz dried elbow macaroni

350 ml/12 fl oz water

Topping

2 thick slices French bread or sourdough bread

2 tbsp butter

Method

1 Line the slow cooker with foil and brush with a little oil.

2 Melt the butter in a large frying pan or saucepan over a medium–high heat. Whisk in the flour and cook for 1 minute. Reduce the heat to medium and slowly add the stock, evaporated milk, mustard powder, cayenne pepper and salt. Cook, stirring, for about 3–5 minutes, until thick. Add all the cheeses and whisk until melted. Add the macaroni and stir to mix well. Transfer to the slow cooker.

3 Add the water and stir to mix. Cover and cook on high for about 2 hours or on low for about 4 hours, until the macaroni is tender.

4 To make the topping, process the bread in a food processor to make crumbs. Melt the butter in a large frying pan over a medium heat until bubbling. Add the breadcrumbs and cook, stirring frequently, for about 5 minutes, until toasted and golden brown.

5 Serve immediately topped with the breadcrumbs.

MEAT-FREE MEALS

BAKED AUBERGINE WITH COURGETTE & TOMATO

Serves: 4

Prep: 20–25 mins

Cook: 4 hours 10 mins

Ingredients

2 large aubergines

olive oil, for brushing

2 large courgettes, sliced

4 tomatoes, sliced

1 garlic clove, finely chopped

15 g/½ oz dry breadcrumbs

15 g/½ oz grated Parmesan cheese

salt and pepper

fresh basil leaves, torn, to garnish

Method

1 Cut the aubergines into fairly thin slices and brush with oil. Heat a large griddle pan or heavy-based frying pan over a high heat, then add the aubergines and cook in batches for 6–8 minutes, turning once, until soft and brown.

2 Layer the aubergines in the slow cooker with the courgettes, tomatoes and garlic, seasoning to taste with salt and pepper between the layers.

3 Mix the breadcrumbs with the cheese and sprinkle over the vegetables. Cover and cook on low for 4 hours. Serve immediately, garnished with basil.

MEAT-FREE MEALS

LENTIL & VEGETABLE CASSEROLE

Serves: 4 **Prep: 25 mins** **Cook: 4½–6 hours**

Ingredients

1 onion

10 cloves

225 g/8 oz Puy or green lentils

1 bay leaf

1.5 litres/2¾ pints vegetable stock

2 leeks, sliced

2 potatoes, diced

2 carrots, chopped

3 courgettes, sliced

1 celery stick, sliced

1 red pepper, deseeded and chopped

1 tbsp lemon juice

salt and pepper

Method

1 Peel the onion, stud it with the cloves and place it in the slow cooker. Add the lentils and bay leaf, pour in the stock, cover and cook on high for 1½ –2 hours.

2 Remove the onion with a slotted spoon and re-cover the slow cooker. Remove and discard the cloves and slice the onion. Add the onion, leeks, potatoes, carrots, courgettes, celery and red pepper to the lentils. Season to taste with salt and pepper, re-cover and cook on high for 3–4 hours until all the vegetables are tender.

3 Remove and discard the bay leaf and stir in the lemon juice. Taste and adjust the seasoning if necessary, then serve immediately.

MEAT-FREE MEALS

WINTER VEGETABLE MEDLEY

Serves: 4   **Prep: 15–20 mins**   **Cook: 3¼ hours**

Ingredients

2 tbsp sunflower oil

2 onions, chopped

3 carrots, chopped

3 parsnips, chopped

2 bunches celery, chopped

2 tbsp chopped
fresh parsley

1 tbsp chopped
fresh coriander

300 ml/10 fl oz vegetable
stock

salt and pepper

Method

1 Heat the oil in a large, heavy-based saucepan. Add the onions and cook over a medium heat, stirring occasionally, for 5 minutes until softened. Add the carrots, parsnips and celery and cook, stirring occasionally, for a further 5 minutes. Stir in the herbs, season to taste with salt and pepper and pour in the stock. Bring to the boil.

2 Transfer the vegetable mixture to the slow cooker, cover and cook on high for 3 hours until tender. Taste and adjust the seasoning if necessary. Using a slotted spoon, transfer the medley to warmed plates, then spoon over a little of the cooking liquid. Serve immediately.

MEAT-FREE MEALS

SUMMER VEGETABLE CASSEROLE

Serves: 4   **Prep: 20 mins**   **Cook: 7 hours**

Ingredients

500 g/1 lb 2 oz potatoes, cubed

2 courgettes, cubed

2 red peppers, deseeded and cubed

2 red onions, sliced

2 tsp mixed dried herbs

250 ml/9 fl oz vegetable stock

salt and pepper

Method

1 Layer all the vegetables in the slow cooker, sprinkling with herbs and salt and pepper to taste between the layers.

2 Pour over the stock. Cover and cook on low for 7 hours. Transfer to warmed serving bowls and serve immediately.

MEAT-FREE MEALS

TOFU WITH SPICY PEANUT SAUCE

Serves: 4　　　　**Prep: 20 mins**　　　　**Cook: 4¼ hours**

Ingredients

675 g/1 lb 8 oz extra-firm tofu

2 tbsp vegetable oil

85 g/3 oz smooth peanut butter

3 tbsp low-sodium soy sauce

3 tbsp unseasoned rice vinegar

juice of 1 lime

2 tbsp soft light brown sugar

2 tsp toasted sesame oil

2 garlic cloves, finely chopped

1 tbsp finely chopped fresh ginger

2 jalapeño chillies, deseeded and finely chopped

350 g/12 oz baby spinach leaves

chopped fresh coriander, to serve

steamed rice, to serve

Method

1 Slice the tofu into 2.5-cm/1-inch thick slabs and pat very dry with kitchen paper, pressing to release any excess moisture. Cut into 2.5-cm/ 1-inch cubes.

2 Heat the vegetable oil in a large, non-stick frying pan over a medium–high heat. Add the tofu, in batches, if necessary, and cook on one side for about 3 minutes, until brown. Turn and cook on the other side for a further 3 minutes, until brown.

3 Meanwhile, put the peanut butter, soy sauce, vinegar, lime juice, sugar, sesame oil, garlic, ginger and chillies into the slow cooker and mix to combine.

4 Add the tofu to the slow cooker. Stir gently to coat, cover and cook on low for about 4 hours.

5 About 15 minutes before serving, place the spinach in the slow cooker on top of the cooked tofu mixture, re-cover and cook for about 15 minutes, until the spinach is wilted. Stir in the coriander and serve immediately with steamed rice.

BUTTERNUT SQUASH & GOAT'S CHEESE ENCHILADAS

Serves: 4　　　　**Prep: 35–40 mins**　　　　**Cook: 2 hours 50 mins–3 hours**

Ingredients

1 large butternut squash, peeled and diced

4 tbsp olive oil

1 tsp salt

3 tsp ground cumin

1 large onion, diced

3 garlic cloves, finely chopped

1 tbsp hot or mild chilli powder

1 tbsp dried oregano

450g/1 lb canned puréed tomatoes or passata

1 tbsp clear honey

450 ml/16 fl oz vegetable stock

12 corn tortillas

225 g/8 oz soft, fresh goat's cheese

Method

1　Preheat the oven to 200°C/400°F/Gas Mark 6. Line a baking tray with baking paper. Coat the squash with 2 tablespoons of the oil, sprinkle with half the salt and 1 teaspoon of the cumin. Place the squash on the tray and roast for 30–40 minutes, until soft and beginning to brown.

2　Heat the remaining oil in a large frying pan over a medium–high heat. Add the onion and garlic and cook, stirring, for about 5 minutes, until soft. Add the remaining cumin and salt, the chilli powder and the oregano and cook for a further 1 minute. Stir in the puréed tomatoes, honey and stock, bring to the boil and cook for about 5 minutes. Purée the sauce in a food processor or blender.

3　Coat the base of the slow cooker with a little sauce. Make a layer of tortillas, tearing them if necessary, to cover the bottom of the slow cooker. Top the tortillas with a layer of the squash, a layer of cheese, a layer of sauce, then another layer of tortillas.

4　Layer again with squash, cheese and sauce. Finish with a layer of tortillas, sauce and the remaining cheese. Cover and cook on low for 2 hours, until the tortillas are soft and the cheese is melted and bubbling. Serve immediately.

PARSLEY DUMPLING STEW

Serves: 6   **Prep: 30 mins**   **Cook: 6½ hours**

Ingredients

½ swede, cut into chunks

2 onions, sliced

2 potatoes, cut into chunks

2 carrots, cut into chunks

2 celery sticks, sliced

2 courgettes, sliced

2 tbsp tomato purée

600 ml/1 pint vegetable stock

1 bay leaf

1 tsp ground coriander

½ tsp dried thyme

400 g/14 oz canned sweetcorn, drained

salt and pepper

Parsley dumplings

200 g/7 oz self-raising flour

pinch of salt

115 g/4 oz vegetable suet

2 tbsp chopped fresh flat-leaf parsley, plus extra sprigs to garnish

about 125 ml/4 fl oz milk

Method

1 Put the swede, onions, potatoes, carrots, celery and courgettes into the slow cooker. Stir the tomato purée into the stock and pour it over the vegetables. Add the bay leaf, coriander and thyme and season to taste with salt and pepper. Cover and cook on low for 6 hours.

2 To make the dumplings, sift the flour with the salt into a bowl and stir in the suet and chopped parsley. Add just enough of the milk to make a firm but light dough. Knead lightly and shape into 12 small balls.

3 Stir the sweetcorn into the mixture in the slow cooker and place the dumplings on top. Re-cover and cook on high for 30 minutes. Remove and discard the bay leaf. Transfer to warmed serving plates, garnish with parsley sprigs and serve immediately.

MIXED BEAN CHILLI

Serves: 4–6

Prep: 30 mins,
plus soaking

Cook: 10¾ hours

Ingredients

115 g/4 oz dried red kidney beans, soaked overnight, drained and rinsed

115 g/4 oz dried black beans, soaked overnight, drained and rinsed

115 g/4 oz dried pinto beans, soaked overnight, drained and rinsed

2 tbsp corn oil

1 onion, chopped

1 garlic clove, finely chopped

1 fresh red chilli, deseeded and chopped

1 yellow pepper, deseeded and chopped

1 tsp ground cumin

1 tbsp chilli powder

1 litre/1¾ pints vegetable stock

1 tbsp sugar

salt and pepper

chopped fresh coriander, to garnish

crusty bread, to serve

Method

1 Place all the beans in a saucepan, cover with fresh cold water and bring to the boil. Boil rapidly for at least 10 minutes, then remove from the heat, drain and rinse again.

2 Heat the oil in a large, heavy-based saucepan. Add the onion, garlic, chilli and yellow pepper and cook over a medium heat, stirring occasionally, for 5 minutes. Stir in the cumin and chilli powder and cook, stirring, for 1–2 minutes. Add the drained beans and stock and bring to the boil. Boil vigorously for 15 minutes.

3 Transfer the mixture to the slow cooker, cover and cook on low for 10 hours, until the beans are tender.

4 Season to taste with salt and pepper, then ladle about one third into a bowl. Mash well with a potato masher, then return the mashed beans to the slow cooker and stir in the sugar. Transfer to warmed serving bowls and garnish with chopped coriander. Serve immediately with crusty bread.

MEAT-FREE MEALS

STUFFED BUTTERNUT SQUASH

Serves: 4   **Prep: 25 mins**   **Cook: 6 hours 35 mins**

Ingredients

2 tbsp olive oil

1 shallot, diced

2 garlic cloves, finely chopped

250 g/9 oz chard, stems and thick centre ribs removed and leaves cut into wide ribbons

¾ tsp salt

1 tsp paprika

450 ml/16 fl oz vegetable stock

175 g/6 oz quinoa

425 g/15 oz canned cannellini beans, rinsed and drained

25 g/1 oz stoned Kalamata olives, diced

115 g/4 oz feta cheese, crumbled

2 tbsp finely chopped fresh mint leaves

2 butternut squash, halved and deseeded

Method

1 Heat the oil in a large frying pan over a medium–high heat. Add the shallot and garlic and cook, stirring, for about 5 minutes, until soft. Add the chard and cook for about 3 minutes, until wilted. Add the salt and paprika and cook for a further 1 minute. Add the stock and quinoa and bring to the boil. Reduce the heat to low, cover and simmer for 15–20 minutes, until the quinoa is cooked through.

2 Stir in the beans, olives, half of the cheese and the mint.

3 Fill the slow cooker with water to a depth of 5 mm/¼ inch. Divide the quinoa mixture between the squash halves, then place them in the slow cooker, stuffed side up. Cover and cook on low for 6 hours.

4 Preheat the grill. Remove the squash halves from the slow cooker and top with the remaining cheese. Cook under the preheated grill for about 3 minutes, until the cheese is beginning to brown. Serve immediately.

WILD MUSHROOM LASAGNE

Serves: 4–6

Prep: 35 mins, plus soaking

Cook: 4 hours 35 mins

Ingredients

vegetable oil, for brushing

225 g/8 oz lasagne sheets

25 g/1 oz freshly grated Parmesan cheese

Filling

25 g/1 oz dried ceps

450 ml/16 fl oz boiling water

2 tbsp olive oil

1 small onion, diced

2 garlic cloves, finely chopped

450 g/1 lb button mushrooms, sliced

125 ml/4 fl oz red wine

1 tbsp finely chopped fresh thyme leaves

½ tsp salt

½ tsp pepper

Sauce

55 g/2 oz unsalted butter

35 g/1¼ oz plain flour

600 ml/1 pint milk

85 g/3 oz freshly grated Parmesan cheese

¾ tsp salt

Method

1 To make the filling, soak the ceps in the water for 30 minutes. Remove the mushrooms, reserving the liquid, and chop. Heat the oil in a large frying pan over a medium–high heat. Add the onion and garlic and cook, stirring, for 5 minutes. Add the fresh and reconstituted mushrooms and cook, stirring, for about 5 minutes, until soft. Add the wine, bring to the boil and cook for about 5 minutes, until the liquid has almost evaporated. Add the mushroom soaking liquid, thyme, salt and pepper and cook over a medium–high heat, stirring frequently, for a further 5 minutes, or until the liquid is reduced by half.

2 To make the sauce, melt the butter in a large saucepan over a medium heat. Whisk in the flour and cook, whisking constantly, for about 3 minutes, until the mixture is golden brown. Whisk in the milk and bring to the boil. Reduce the heat and simmer for 3 minutes, then remove from the heat and stir in the cheese and salt.

3 To assemble the lasagne, line the slow cooker with foil, overlapping two large pieces to cover the entire base. Lightly brush the foil with oil. Spoon a thin layer of sauce and a thin layer of mushrooms over the base.

MEAT-FREE MEALS

4 Top with a layer of pasta. Repeat, to make a total of three layers. Top with a final layer of pasta, then a layer of sauce. Sprinkle the cheese over the top. Cover and cook on low for about 4 hours, until the pasta is tender and the top is brown and bubbling. Serve the lasagne directly from the slow cooker or use the foil as a sling to lift it out to serve.

VEGETARIAN PAELLA

Serves: 6 **Prep: 25 mins** **Cook: 2¾–3¼ hours**

Ingredients

4 tbsp olive oil

1 Spanish onion, sliced

2 garlic cloves, finely chopped

1 litre/1¾ pints vegetable stock

large pinch of saffron threads, lightly crushed

1 yellow pepper, deseeded and sliced

1 red pepper, deseeded and sliced

1 large aubergine, diced

225 g/8 oz paella or risotto rice

450 g/1 lb tomatoes, peeled and chopped

115 g/4 oz chestnut mushrooms, sliced

115 g/4 oz French beans, halved

400 g/14 oz canned borlotti beans, drained and rinsed

salt and pepper

Method

1 Heat the oil in a large frying pan. Add the onion and garlic and cook over a low heat, stirring occasionally, for 5 minutes, until softened. Put 3 tablespoons of the hot stock into a small bowl and stir in the saffron, then set aside to infuse.

2 Add the peppers and aubergine to the pan and cook, stirring occasionally, for 5 minutes. Add the rice and cook, stirring constantly, for 1 minute, until the grains are coated with oil and glistening. Pour in the remaining stock and add the tomatoes, mushrooms, French beans and borlotti beans. Stir in the saffron mixture and season to taste with salt and pepper.

3 Transfer the mixture to the slow cooker, cover and cook on low for 2½–3 hours, until the rice is tender and the stock has been absorbed. Transfer to warmed serving plates and serve immediately.

SPAGHETTI WITH LENTIL BOLOGNESE SAUCE

Serves: 4–6　　　　**Prep: 20 mins**　　　　**Cook: 8¼ hours**

Ingredients

2 tbsp olive oil

1 onion, diced

2 garlic cloves, finely chopped

1 carrot, diced

2 celery sticks, diced

4 large mushrooms, diced

1 tbsp tomato purée

1 tsp salt

1 tsp crumbled dried oregano

1 bay leaf

400 g/14 oz canned chopped tomatoes, with juice

50 g/1¾ oz dried lentils

225 ml/8 fl oz water

450 g/1 lb dried spaghetti

Method

1　Heat the oil in a large frying pan over a medium–high heat. Add the onion and garlic and cook, stirring, for about 5 minutes, until soft. Add the carrot, celery and mushrooms and continue to cook, stirring occasionally, for a further 5 minutes, or until the mushrooms are soft. Stir in the tomato purée, salt, oregano and bay leaf and cook, stirring, for a further 1 minute. Transfer the mixture to the slow cooker.

2　Stir in the tomatoes with their can juices, lentils and water. Cover and cook on high for 8 hours.

3　Just before serving, cook the spaghetti according to the packet instructions. Transfer the spaghetti to warmed serving dishes and spoon the hot sauce over. Serve immediately.

MEAT-FREE MEALS

VEGETABLE CURRY

Serves: 4-6 **Prep: 25 mins** **Cook: 5 hours 25 mins**

Ingredients

2 tbsp vegetable oil

1 tsp cumin seeds

1 onion, sliced

2 curry leaves

2.5-cm/1-inch piece fresh ginger, finely chopped

2 fresh red chillies, deseeded and chopped

2 tbsp Indian curry paste

2 carrots, sliced

115 g/4 oz mangetout

1 cauliflower, cut into florets

3 tomatoes, peeled and chopped

85 g/3 oz frozen peas

½ tsp ground turmeric

150–225 ml/5–8 fl oz vegetable stock

salt and pepper

Method

1 Heat the oil in a large heavy-based saucepan. Add the cumin seeds and cook, stirring constantly, for 1–2 minutes, until they give off their aroma and begin to pop. Add the onion and curry leaves and cook, stirring occasionally, for 5 minutes, until the onion has softened. Add the ginger and chillies and cook, stirring occasionally, for 1 minute.

2 Stir in the curry paste and cook, stirring, for 2 minutes, then add the carrots, mangetout and cauliflower. Cook for 5 minutes, then add the tomatoes, peas and turmeric and season to taste with salt and pepper. Cook for 3 minutes, then add 150 ml/5 fl oz of the stock and bring to the boil.

3 Transfer the mixture to the slow cooker. If the vegetables are not covered by the liquid, add more hot stock, then cover and cook on low for 5 hours, until tender. Remove and discard the curry leaves. Transfer to warmed serving dishes and serve immediately.

MEAT-FREE MEALS

SPRING VEGETABLES

Serves: 4

Prep: 25 mins,
plus soaking

Cook: 3½–4½ hours

Ingredients

2 tbsp olive oil

4–8 baby onions, halved

2 celery sticks, cut into
5-mm/¼-inch slices

225 g/8 oz young carrots,
halved if large

300 g/10½ oz new potatoes,
halved

850 ml–1.2 litres/1½–2 pints
vegetable stock

225 g/8 oz dried haricot
beans, soaked overnight in
cold water and drained

1 bouquet garni

1½–2 tbsp light soy sauce

85 g/3 oz baby sweetcorn

115 g/4 oz shelled broad
beans, thawed if frozen

225 g/8 oz Savoy cabbage,
shredded

1½ tbsp cornflour

salt and pepper

55–85 g/2–3 oz freshly
grated Parmesan cheese,
to serve

Method

1 Heat the oil in a saucepan. Add the onions,
celery, carrots and potatoes and cook over a
low heat, stirring frequently, for 5–8 minutes until
softened. Add the stock, haricot beans, bouquet
garni and soy sauce, bring to the boil, then
transfer to the slow cooker.

2 Add the corn, broad beans and cabbage,
season to taste with salt and pepper and stir well.
Cover and cook on high for 3–4 hours until the
vegetables are tender.

3 Remove and discard the bouquet garni. Stir the
cornflour with 3 tablespoons of water to a paste
in a small bowl, then stir into the stew. Re-cover
and cook on high for a further 15 minutes until
thickened. Serve the stew immediately with the
Parmesan handed separately.

PUMPKIN RISOTTO

Serves: 4   **Prep: 20 mins**   **Cook: 1 hour 55 mins**

Ingredients

2 tbsp olive oil

1 shallot, finely chopped

1 garlic clove, finely chopped

280 g/10 oz arborio rice

125 ml/4 fl oz dry white wine

1.2 litres/2 pints vegetable stock

425 g/15 oz canned pumpkin purée

1 tbsp finely chopped fresh sage

½ tsp salt

¼ tsp pepper

pinch of nutmeg

2 tbsp butter

115 g/4 oz freshly grated Parmesan cheese, plus extra to serve

Method

1 Heat the oil in a large frying pan over a medium–high heat. Add the shallot and garlic and cook, stirring, for about 5 minutes, until soft. Add the rice and cook, stirring, for 1 minute. Add the wine and cook for a further 3 minutes, until the liquid is absorbed. Transfer the mixture to the slow cooker.

2 Stir in the stock, pumpkin purée, sage, salt, pepper and nutmeg. Cover and cook on high for about 1½ hours, until the rice is tender. Stir in the butter, re-cover and cook for a further 15 minutes. Stir in the cheese and serve immediately, with a little more cheese sprinkled over.

ASPARAGUS & SPINACH RISOTTO

Serves: 4   **Prep: 20 mins**   **Cook: 2 hours 35 mins**

Ingredients

2 tbsp olive oil

4 shallots, finely chopped

280 g/10 oz arborio rice

1 garlic clove, crushed

100 ml/3½ fl oz dry white wine

850 ml/1½ pints vegetable stock

200 g/7 oz asparagus spears

200 g/7 oz baby spinach leaves

40 g/1½ oz freshly grated Parmesan cheese

salt and pepper

Method

1 Heat the oil in a frying pan, add the shallots and fry over a medium heat, stirring, for 2–3 minutes. Add the rice and garlic and cook for a further 2 minutes, stirring. Add the wine and allow it to boil for 30 seconds.

2 Transfer the rice mixture to the slow cooker, add the stock and season to taste with salt and pepper. Cover and cook on high for 2 hours, or until most of the liquid is absorbed.

3 Cut the asparagus into 4-cm/1½-inch lengths. Stir into the rice, then spread the spinach over the top. Re-cover and cook on high for a further 30 minutes, until the asparagus is just tender and the spinach is wilted.

4 Stir in the cheese, then adjust the seasoning to taste and serve immediately in warmed bowls.

WHITE BEAN STEW

Serves: 4   **Prep: 25 mins**   **Cook: 3 hours 20 mins–
6 hours 20 mins**

Ingredients

2 tbsp olive oil

1 onion, diced

2 garlic cloves, finely
chopped

2 carrots, diced

2 celery sticks, diced

175 g/6 oz canned tomato
purée

1 tsp salt

½ tsp pepper

¼–½ tsp crushed dried red
pepper flakes

1 bay leaf

225 ml/8 fl oz dry white wine

850 g/1 lb 14 oz canned
cannellini beans, rinsed
and drained

250 g/9 oz chard, kale or
other winter greens, stems
and thick centre ribs
removed, leaves cut into
wide ribbons

225 ml/8 fl oz water

25 g/1 oz freshly grated
Parmesan cheese, to serve

Method

1 Heat the oil in a large frying pan over a
medium–high heat. Add the onion and garlic
and cook, stirring, for about 5 minutes, until soft.
Add the carrots and celery and cook for a
further few minutes. Stir in the tomato purée,
salt, pepper, red pepper flakes and bay leaf,
then add the wine.

2 Bring to the boil and cook, stirring and scraping
up any sediment from the base of the pan, for
about 5 minutes, until most of the liquid has
evaporated. Transfer the mixture to the
slow cooker.

3 Stir in the beans, chard and water. Cover and
cook on high for 3 hours or on low for 6 hours.
Remove and discard the bay leaf. Serve the stew
hot, garnished with the cheese.

★ Variation

You can use any beans in this tasty stew – from
chickpeas to haricot beans. Ensure that any
dried beans are soaked as per the packet
instructions before using.

MEAT-FREE MEALS

DESSERTS, PUDDINGS & BAKES

DOUBLE CHOCOLATE COOKIES

Makes: 18

Prep: 20 mins,
plus cooling

Cook: 3 hours

Ingredients

125 g/4½ oz plain flour

85 g/3 oz cocoa powder

½ tsp baking powder

¼ tsp salt

115 g/4 oz unsalted butter, softened, plus extra for greasing

100 g/3½ oz sugar

1 large egg

1 tsp vanilla extract

25 g/1 oz plain chocolate chips

Method

1 Generously grease the inside of the slow cooker with butter.

2 Put the flour, cocoa powder, baking powder and salt into a medium-sized bowl and mix to combine. Put the butter and sugar into a large bowl and cream together. Add the egg and vanilla extract and beat well together. Gradually beat in the flour mixture until well incorporated. Stir in the chocolate chips.

3 Using a rubber spatula, scrape the batter into the prepared slow cooker and smooth the top. Cover and cook on low for 2½ hours. Set the lid slightly ajar and continue to cook on low for a further 30 minutes.

4 Leaving the cookie in the ceramic insert, remove it from the slow cooker and transfer to a wire rack to cool for 30 minutes. Turn the cookie out onto the rack and leave to cool for a further 30 minutes before slicing it into 5-cm/2-inch pieces. Serve at room temperature.

★ Variation

Why not add a little crunch to your cookies and add 25 g/1 oz of mixed chopped nuts instead of the chocolate chips. For an even greater treat – use both!

CHOCOLATE & WALNUT SPONGE

Serves: 4   **Prep: 25 mins**   **Cook: 3–3½ hours**

Ingredients

55 g/2 oz cocoa powder, plus extra for dusting

2 tbsp milk

115 g/4 oz self-raising flour

pinch of salt

115 g/4 oz unsalted butter, softened, plus extra for greasing

115 g/4 oz caster sugar

2 eggs, lightly beaten

55 g/2 oz walnut halves, chopped

whipped cream, to serve

Method

1 Grease a 1.2-litre/2-pint pudding basin with butter. Cut out a double round of greaseproof paper that is 7 cm/2¾ inches wider than the rim of the basin. Grease one side with butter and make a pleat in the centre.

2 Mix the cocoa and the milk to a paste in a small bowl. Sift together the flour and salt into a separate small bowl. Set aside.

3 Beat together the butter and sugar in a large bowl until pale and fluffy. Gradually beat in the eggs, a little at a time, then gently fold in the sifted flour mixture, followed by the cocoa mixture and the walnuts.

4 Spoon the mixture into the prepared basin. Cover the basin with the greaseproof paper rounds, buttered-side down, and tie in place with string. Stand the basin on a trivet in the slow cooker and pour in enough boiling water to come about halfway up the side of the basin. Cover and cook on high for 3–3½ hours.

5 Remove the basin from the slow cooker and discard the greaseproof paper. Run a knife around the inside of the basin, then turn out onto a warmed serving dish. Serve with whipped cream, dusted with cocoa.

POACHED PEACHES IN MARSALA

Serves: 4

Prep: 20 mins, plus cooling & optional chilling

Cook: 1 hour 20 mins– 1 hour 50 mins

Ingredients

150 ml/5 fl oz Marsala

175 ml/6 fl oz water

4 tbsp caster sugar

1 vanilla pod, split lengthways

6 peaches, stoned and cut into wedges or 12 apricots, stoned and halved

2 tsp cornflour

crème fraîche or Greek yogurt, to serve

Method

1 Pour the Marsala and 150 ml/5 fl oz of the water into a saucepan and add the sugar and vanilla pod. Set the pan over a low heat and stir until the sugar has dissolved, then bring to the boil without stirring. Remove from the heat.

2 Put the peaches into the slow cooker and pour the syrup over them. Cover and cook on high for 1–1½ hours, until the fruit is tender.

3 Using a slotted spoon, gently transfer the peaches to a serving dish. Remove the vanilla pod from the slow cooker and scrape the seeds into the syrup with the point of a knife. Discard the pod. Stir the cornflour to a paste with the remaining water in a small bowl, then stir into the syrup. Re-cover and cook on high for 15 minutes, stirring occasionally.

4 Spoon the syrup over the fruit and leave to cool slightly. Serve warm or chill in the refrigerator for 2 hours before serving with crème fraîche or yogurt.

BLUSHING PEARS

Serves: 6

Prep: 20 mins, plus cooling & chilling

Cook: 4 hours

Ingredients

6 small ripe pears

225 ml/8 fl oz ruby port

200 g/7 oz caster sugar

1 tsp finely chopped crystallized ginger

2 tbsp lemon juice

whipped cream or Greek yogurt, to serve

Method

1 Peel the pears, cut them in half lengthways and scoop out the cores. Place them in the slow cooker.

2 Combine the port, sugar, ginger and lemon juice in a jug and pour the mixture over the pears. Cover and cook on low for 4 hours, until the pears are tender.

3 Leave the pears to cool in the slow cooker, then carefully transfer to a bowl and chill in the refrigerator until required.

4 To serve, cut each pear half into about six slices lengthways, leaving the fruit intact at the stalk end. Carefully lift the pear halves onto serving plates and press gently to fan out the slices. Spoon the cooking juices over the pears and serve immediately with whipped cream.

DESSERTS, PUDDINGS & BAKES

STUFFED APPLES

Serves: 4   **Prep: 20 mins**   **Cook: 1½–3 hours**

Ingredients

4 large cooking apples

175 g/6 oz soft light brown sugar

25 g/1 oz rolled oats

1 tsp ground cinnamon

4 tbsp butter, cut into small pieces

2 tbsp sultanas

25 g/1 oz pecan nuts or walnuts, roughly chopped

whipped cream, to serve

Method

1 Use a paring knife to cut the stem end out of each apple, then scoop out the core with a melon baller or teaspoon, leaving the base of the apple intact.

2 To make the filling, put the sugar, oats, cinnamon and butter into a bowl and mix together with a fork. Add the sultanas and nuts and toss to mix well. Stuff the mixture into the apples, dividing it evenly.

3 Pour 125 ml/4 fl oz of water into the slow cooker, then carefully add the apples, standing them up in the base of the slow cooker. Cover and cook on high for about 1½ hours or on low for 3 hours. Serve the apples hot, topped with whipped cream.

DESSERTS, PUDDINGS & BAKES

RICE PUDDING

Serves: 4 **Prep: 15 mins** **Cook: 2¼ hours–2 hours 20 mins**

Ingredients

140 g/5 oz short-grain rice
1 litre/1¾ pints milk
115 g/4 oz sugar
1 tsp vanilla extract
ground cinnamon,
for dusting

Method

1 Rinse the rice well under cold running water and drain thoroughly. Pour the milk into a large heavy-based saucepan, add the sugar and bring to the boil, stirring constantly. Sprinkle in the rice, stir well and simmer gently for 10–15 minutes. Transfer the mixture to a heatproof dish and cover with foil.

2 Stand the dish on a trivet in the slow cooker and pour in enough boiling water to come about one third of the way up the side of the dish. Cover and cook on high for 2 hours.

3 Remove the dish from the slow cooker and discard the foil. Stir the vanilla extract into the rice, then spoon it into warmed bowls. Lightly dust with cinnamon and serve immediately.

CHOCOLATE POTS

Serves: 6

Prep: 25 mins, plus cooling & chilling

Cook: 3 hours 10 mins-3 hours 40 mins

Ingredients

300 ml/10 fl oz single cream

300 ml/10 fl oz milk

225 g/8 oz plain chocolate, broken into small pieces

1 large egg

4 egg yolks

4 tbsp caster sugar

150 ml/5 fl oz double cream

grated chocolate, to decorate

Method

1 Pour the single cream and milk into a saucepan and add the chocolate. Set the pan over a very low heat and stir until the chocolate has melted and the mixture is smooth. Remove from the heat and leave to cool for 10 minutes.

2 Beat together the egg, egg yolks and sugar in a bowl until combined. Gradually stir in the chocolate mixture until thoroughly blended, then strain into a jug.

3 Divide the mixture between six ramekins and cover with foil. Stand the ramekins on a trivet in the slow cooker and pour in enough boiling water to come about halfway up the sides of the ramekins. Cover and cook on low for 3–3½ hours, until just set. Remove the slow cooker pot from the base and leave to cool completely. Remove the ramekins and chill in the refrigerator for at least 4 hours.

4 Whip the double cream in a bowl until it holds soft peaks. Top each chocolate pot with a little of the whipped cream and decorate with grated chocolate. Serve immediately.

BUTTERSCOTCH PUDDINGS

Serves: 6

Prep: 20 mins, plus cooling & chilling

Cook: 2 hours 5 mins

Ingredients

2 tbsp unsalted butter

275 g/9¾ oz soft dark brown sugar

½ tsp salt

300 ml/10 fl oz double cream

175 ml/6 fl oz milk

4 egg yolks, lightly beaten

2 tsp vanilla extract

2 tsp whisky

whipped cream, to serve

Method

1 Fill the slow cooker with water to a depth of about 4 cm/1½ inches.

2 Melt the butter in a large saucepan over a medium heat. Add the sugar and salt and stir to mix well. Add the cream and milk and heat over a medium heat, until hot but not boiling.

3 Place the egg yolks in a medium-sized mixing bowl. Add the sugar and milk mixture in a very thin stream, whisking constantly. Whisk in the vanilla extract and whisky. Ladle the mixture into six 125-ml/4-fl oz ramekins.

4 Carefully place the ramekins in the slow cooker, taking care not to slosh any of the water into them. Cover the slow cooker and cook on low for about 2 hours, or until the puddings are set.

5 Remove the ramekins from the slow cooker and transfer to a wire rack to cool for about 15 minutes, then cover with clingfilm, place in the refrigerator and chill for at least 2 hours before serving. Serve chilled, topped with a dollop of whipped cream.

ALMOND CHARLOTTE

Serves: 4 **Prep: 25–30 mins** **Cook: 3 hours 10 mins–3 hours 40 mins, plus standing**

Ingredients

unsalted butter, for greasing

10–12 sponge fingers

300 ml/10 fl oz milk

2 eggs

2 tbsp caster sugar

55 g/2 oz blanched almonds, chopped

4–5 drops of almond extract

Sherry sauce

1 tbsp caster sugar

3 egg yolks

150 ml/5 fl oz cream sherry

Method

1 Grease a 600-ml/1-pint pudding basin with butter. Line the basin with the sponge fingers, cutting them to fit and placing them cut-sides down and sugar-coated sides outwards. Cover the base with some of the offcuts.

2 Pour the milk into a saucepan and bring just to the boil, then remove from the heat. Beat together the eggs and sugar in a heatproof bowl until combined, then stir in the milk. Stir in the almonds and almond extract.

3 Carefully pour the mixture into the prepared basin and cover with foil. Stand the basin on a trivet in the slow cooker and pour in enough boiling water to come about halfway up the side of the dish. Cover and cook on high for 3–3½ hours, until set.

4 To make the sherry sauce, put the sugar, egg yolks and sherry into a heatproof bowl. Set the bowl over a pan of simmering water. Whisk well until the mixture thickens, but do not boil. Remove from the heat.

5 Carefully remove the basin from the slow cooker and discard the foil. Leave to stand for 2–3 minutes, then turn out onto a warmed serving plate. Pour the sherry sauce around it and serve immediately.

STEAMED SPONGE WITH TOFFEE SAUCE

Serves: 6 **Prep: 25–30 mins** **Cook: 3 hours 5 mins–3 hours 20 mins**

Ingredients

115 g/4 oz toasted hazelnuts, chopped

115 g/4 oz unsalted butter, plus extra for greasing

115 g/4 oz soft dark brown sugar

2 eggs, lightly beaten

115 g/4 oz self-raising flour

1 tbsp lemon juice

Toffee sauce

55 g/2 oz unsalted butter

55 g/2 oz soft dark brown sugar

4 tbsp double cream

1 tbsp lemon juice

Method

1 Grease an 850-ml/1½-pint pudding basin with butter and sprinkle half the nuts over the base. Cut out a double round of greaseproof paper that is 7 cm/2¾ inches wider than the rim of the basin. Make a pleat in the centre.

2 To make the sauce, put all of the ingredients into a saucepan over a low heat. Stir until the mixture is smooth and thoroughly combined. Remove from the heat, pour half the sauce into the basin and swirl gently to coat the sides. Reserve the remainder.

3 Beat together the butter and sugar in a bowl until light and fluffy. Gradually beat in the eggs, then gently fold in the flour, lemon juice and the remaining hazelnuts. Spoon the mixture into the basin. Cover the basin with the greaseproof paper rounds and tie in place with string.

4 Stand the basin on a trivet in the slow cooker and pour in enough boiling water to come about halfway up the side of the basin. Cover and cook on high for 3–3¼ hours, until just set.

5 Just before serving, gently reheat the reserved sauce. Remove the basin from the slow cooker and discard the greaseproof paper. Run a knife around the inside of the basin and turn out onto a plate. Pour the sauce over and serve.

DESSERTS, PUDDINGS & BAKES

MAGIC LEMON SPONGE

Serves: 4 **Prep: 20 mins** **Cook: 2½ hours**

Ingredients

140 g/5 oz caster sugar

3 eggs, separated

300 ml/10 fl oz milk

3 tbsp self-raising flour, sifted

150 ml/5 fl oz freshly squeezed lemon juice

icing sugar, for dusting

Method

1 Beat the sugar with the egg yolks in a bowl, using an electric mixer. Gradually beat in the milk, followed by the flour and the lemon juice.

2 Whisk the egg whites in a separate, grease-free bowl until stiff. Fold half the whites into the yolk mixture using a rubber or plastic spatula in a figure-of-eight movement, then fold in the remainder. Try not to knock out the air.

3 Pour the mixture into an ovenproof dish, cover with foil and place in the slow cooker. Add sufficient boiling water to come about one-third of the way up the side of the dish. Cover and cook on high for 2½ hours until the mixture has set and the sauce and sponge have separated.

4 Lift the dish out of the cooker and discard the foil. Lightly sift a little icing sugar over the top and serve immediately.

DESSERTS, PUDDINGS & BAKES

CARROT CAKE

Serves: 8–10

Prep: 25 mins,
plus cooling

Cook: 2 hours

Ingredients

125 g/4½ oz plain flour

1 tsp bicarbonate of soda

¼ tsp salt

½ tsp ground cinnamon

pinch of ground nutmeg

2 large eggs

100 g/3½ oz granulated sugar

55 g/2 oz soft light brown sugar

4 tbsp vegetable oil, plus extra for greasing

150 ml/5 fl oz buttermilk

1 tsp vanilla extract

450 g/1 lb carrots, grated

60 g/2¼ oz desiccated coconut

35 g/1¼ oz sultanas

whipped cream, to serve

Method

1 Grease the inside of the slow cooker with oil.

2 Put the flour, bicarbonate of soda, salt, cinnamon and nutmeg into a small bowl and mix to combine. Put the eggs, granulated sugar and brown sugar into a medium-sized bowl and whisk together until well combined. Add the oil, buttermilk and vanilla extract and stir to combine. Add the egg mixture to the flour mixture and mix well. Fold in the carrots, coconut and sultanas.

3 Pour the mixture into the prepared slow cooker. Place several sheets of kitchen paper on top of the slow cooker, then put the lid on top to secure the kitchen paper in place above the cake mixture. Cook on low for about 2 hours, until a skewer inserted into the centre of the cake comes out clean.

4 Leaving the cake in the ceramic insert, remove it from the slow cooker and transfer to a wire rack to cool for at least 30 minutes. Cut the cake into wedges and serve it directly from the insert. Serve warm or at room temperature with a dollop of whipped cream.

DESSERTS, PUDDINGS & BAKES

THAI BLACK RICE PUDDING

Serves: 4

Prep: 20 mins

**Cook: 2 hours 20 mins–
2 hours 50 mins**

Ingredients

175 g/6 oz black glutinous rice

2 tbsp soft light brown sugar

450 ml/16 fl oz canned coconut milk

225 ml/8 fl oz water

3 eggs

2 tbsp caster sugar

Method

1 Mix together the rice, brown sugar and half the coconut milk in a saucepan, then stir in the water. Bring to the boil, then reduce the heat and simmer, stirring occasionally, for 15 minutes, until almost all the liquid has been absorbed. Transfer the mixture into 4 individual ovenproof dishes or 1 large dish.

2 Lightly beat the eggs with the remaining coconut milk and the caster sugar. Strain, then pour the mixture over the rice.

3 Cover the dishes with foil and stand on a trivet in the slow cooker and pour in enough boiling water to come about one third of the way up the sides of the dish. Cover and cook on high for 2–2½ hours, until set. Carefully remove the dishes from the slow cooker and discard the foil. Serve hot or cold.

DESSERTS, PUDDINGS & BAKES

BROWN SUGAR APPLE CAKE

Serves: 6-8　　　　**Prep: 10 mins**　　　　**Cook: 2 hours 30 mins–3 hours**

Ingredients

185 g/6½ oz self-raising flour

½ tsp ground cinnamon

pinch of salt

114 g/4 oz unsalted butter, softenend, plus extra for greasing

225 g/8 oz soft light brown sugar

2 large eggs, lightly beaten

1 tsp vanilla extract

1 medium cooking apple, peeled, cored and finely diced

whipped cream, to serve

Method

1 Grease the inside of the slow cooker with butter.

2 Sift the flour, cinnamon and salt into a medium-sized bowl. Put the butter and sugar into a large bowl and cream together with a hand-held electric mixer.

3 Add the eggs and vanilla extract and beat on high for 1-2 minutes. Fold in the flour mixture using a metal spoon, then gently fold through the diced apple.

4 Spoon the mixture into the prepared slow cooker and level the surface. Cover and cook on low for 2 hours 30 minutes–3 hours, or until the cake is risen, springy to the touch and a skewer inserted into the centre of the cake comes out clean.

5 Leaving the cake in the ceramic insert, remove it from the slow cooker and transfer to a wire rack to cool for at least 1 hour. Run a flexible palette knife around the outside of the cake and underneath it to release it from the insert then carefully turn it out onto a serving platter. Serve with a dollop of whipped cream.

★ Variation

Replace the apple with one small pear, cored and finely diced, and 100g dried, pitted chopped dates.

DESSERTS, PUDDINGS & BAKES

CARAMELIZED
BANANA UPSIDE-DOWN CAKE

Serves: 6–8

Prep: 25 mins,
plus cooling

Cook: 2 hours 2 mins,
plus standing

Ingredients

175 g/6 oz plain flour

55 g/2 oz soft light brown sugar

150 g/5½ oz granulated sugar

¾ tsp bicarbonate of soda

½ tsp baking powder

½ tsp salt

3 tbsp unsalted butter

2 ripe bananas

125 ml/4 fl oz buttermilk

1 tsp vanilla extract

2 eggs

Caramelized banana

5 tbsp unsalted butter

175 g/6 oz soft light brown sugar

pinch of salt

2 small ripe bananas, sliced

Method

1 To make the caramelized banana, put the butter into an 18-cm/7-inch soufflé dish and place it in the microwave on high for about 1 minute, until melted. Tilt the dish to coat the sides and base with the butter, then stir in the sugar and the salt. Spread the mixture evenly over the base of the dish. Add the sliced bananas on top, ideally in a single layer, or overlapping slightly if necessary.

2 Put the first 6 ingredients into a medium-sized bowl and mix to combine. Put the butter into a large bowl and place it in the microwave on high for about 1 minute, until melted. Add the bananas and mash them into the butter. Whisk in the buttermilk, vanilla extract and eggs. Add the flour mixture to the butter mixture and whisk until thoroughly combined.

3 Pour the cake mixture over the sliced bananas in the soufflé dish and place in the slow cooker on a trivet. Cover and cook on low for 2 hours, until cooked through. Turn off the cooker and leave the cake in it for a further 30 minutes.

4 Leave the soufflé dish in the ceramic insert, remove them both from the slow cooker and transfer to a wire rack to cool for 15 minutes. Run a thin knife around the edge of the cake to release it from the sides of the dish, then turn it out onto a large plate to serve.

DESSERTS, PUDDINGS & BAKES

CHOCOLATE CAKE

Serves: 8

Prep: 20 mins,
plus cooling

Cook: 2 hours 40 mins,
plus standing

Ingredients

375 g/13 oz plain chocolate, broken into pieces

175 g/6 oz unsalted butter, plus extra for greasing

175 g/6 oz light muscovado sugar

4 eggs

2 tsp vanilla extract

150 g/5½ oz self-raising flour

55 g/2 oz ground almonds

125 ml/4 fl oz double cream

icing sugar, for dusting

Method

1 Place a trivet in the base of the slow cooker. Grease and base-line a 20-cm/8-inch diameter, deep cake tin, or a tin that fits into your slow cooker.

2 Melt 250 g/9 oz of chocolate in a bowl over a pan of simmering water. Remove from the heat and cool slightly.

3 Beat the butter and sugar in a large bowl until pale and fluffy. Gradually beat in the eggs. Stir in the melted chocolate and 1 teaspoon of vanilla extract. Fold in the flour and almonds evenly.

4 Spoon the mixture into the tin, spreading evenly. Place in the slow cooker, cover and cook on high for 2½ hours or until risen and springy to the touch.

5 Remove from the slow cooker and leave the cake in the tin for 10 minutes. Turn out and cool on a wire rack.

6 Place the remaining chocolate and vanilla extract with the cream in a pan and heat gently, stirring, until melted. Cool until thick enough to spread. Split the cake into two layers and sandwich together with the filling. Dust with icing sugar to serve.

GINGER CAKE

Serves: 8–10

Prep: 20 mins,
plus cooling

Cook: 3 hours 5 mins

Ingredients

115 g/4 oz unsalted butter, melted, plus extra for greasing

85 g/3 oz soft light brown sugar

150 ml/5 fl oz golden syrup

1 tsp vanilla extract

175 g/6 oz plain flour

2 tsp ground ginger

1½ tsp bicarbonate of soda

pinch of salt

2 large eggs, lightly beaten

125 ml/4 fl oz milk

whipped cream, to serve

Method

1 Grease the base and sides of an 18-cm/7-inch soufflé dish. Fill the slow cooker with hot (not boiling) water to a depth of about 2.5 cm/1 inch.

2 Put the butter, sugar, golden syrup and vanilla extract into a medium-sized bowl and stir to mix well. Put the flour, ginger, bicarbonate of soda, and salt into a large mixing bowl and stir to combine. Stir the butter mixture into the flour mixture with a wooden spoon and mix together until well combined. Add the eggs and milk and continue to mix until smooth.

3 Pour the mixture into the prepared soufflé dish and carefully place it in the slow cooker. Cover and cook on low for about 3 hours, until a skewer inserted into the centre of the cake comes out clean. Leave the soufflé dish in the ceramic insert, remove them both from the slow cooker and transfer to a wire rack to cool for at least 30 minutes, then remove the soufflé dish from the insert and leave to cool for a further 30 minutes.

4 To serve, slice the cake into wedges and top with a dollop of whipped cream.

CRÈME BRÛLÉE

Serves: 6

Prep: 20 mins,
plus infusing, cooling
& chilling

**Cook: 3 hours 5 mins–
3 hours 35 mins**

Ingredients

1 vanilla pod
1 litre/1¾ pints double
cream
6 egg yolks
100 g/3½ oz caster sugar
85 g/3 oz soft light
brown sugar

Method

1 Using a sharp knife, split the vanilla pod in
half lengthways, scrape the seeds into a
saucepan and add the pod. Pour in the cream
and bring just to the boil, stirring constantly.
Remove from the heat, cover and leave to
infuse for 20 minutes.

2 Whisk together the egg yolks and caster sugar
in a bowl until thoroughly mixed. Remove and
discard the vanilla pod from the pan, then whisk
the cream into the egg yolk mixture. Strain the
mixture into a large jug.

3 Divide the mixture between 6 ramekins and
cover with foil. Stand the ramekins on a trivet
in the slow cooker and pour in enough boiling
water to come about halfway up the sides of the
ramekins. Cover and cook on low for 3–3½ hours,
until just set. Remove the ceramic insert from
the slow cooker and leave to cool completely.
Remove the ramekins and chill in the refrigerator
for at least 4 hours.

4 Preheat the grill. Sprinkle the brown sugar evenly
over the surface of each dessert, then cook
under the grill for 30–60 seconds, until the sugar
has melted and caramelized. Alternatively, you
can use a cook's blowtorch. Chill for a further
hour before serving.

APPLE CRUMBLE

Serves: 4–6 **Prep: 20 mins** **Cook: 3–5 hours**

Ingredients

100 g/3½ oz sugar

1 tbsp cornflour

1 tsp ground cinnamon

¼ tsp ground nutmeg

6 large cooking apples, peeled, cored and chopped

2 tbsp lemon juice

vanilla ice cream, to serve (optional)

Topping

60 g/2¼ oz plain flour

75 g/2¾ oz soft light brown sugar

3 tbsp granulated sugar

pinch of salt

3 tbsp unsalted butter, cut into small pieces

60 g/2¼ oz rolled oats

85 g/3 oz pecan nuts or walnuts, roughly chopped

Method

1 Put the sugar, cornflour, cinnamon and nutmeg into the slow cooker and stir to combine. Add the apples and lemon juice and toss to coat well.

2 To make the topping, put the flour, brown sugar, granulated sugar and salt into a large mixing bowl and mix to combine. Using two knives, cut the butter into the flour mixture until it resembles coarse crumbs. Add the oats and nuts and toss until well combined.

3 Sprinkle the topping evenly over the apple mixture, cover and cook on high for about 2 hours or on low for about 4 hours, until the apples are soft. Set the lid ajar and cook for a further 1 hour, or until the topping is crisp. Serve warm, topped with vanilla ice cream, if using.

ITALIAN BREAD PUDDING

Serves: 4

Prep: 20 mins, plus cooling & chilling

Cook: 2 hours 35 mins

Ingredients

unsalted butter, for greasing

6 slices panettone

3 tbsp Marsala

300 ml/10 fl oz milk

300 ml/10 fl oz single cream

100 g/3½ oz caster sugar

grated rind of ½ lemon

pinch of ground cinnamon

3 large eggs, lightly beaten

Method

1 Grease a pudding basin and set aside. Place the panettone on a deep plate and sprinkle with the Marsala wine.

2 Pour the milk and cream into a saucepan and add the sugar, lemon rind and cinnamon. Gradually bring to the boil over a low heat, stirring until the sugar has dissolved. Remove the pan from the heat and leave to cool slightly, then pour the mixture onto the eggs, beating constantly.

3 Place the panettone in the prepared dish, pour in the egg mixture and cover with foil. Place in the slow cooker and add enough boiling water to come about one-third of the way up the side of the dish. Cover and cook on high for 2½ hours until set.

4 Remove the dish from the slow cooker and discard the foil. Leave to cool, then chill in the refrigerator until required. Loosen the sides of the pudding and turn out onto a serving dish.

STRAWBERRY CHEESECAKE

Serves: 6–8

Prep: 20 mins,
plus cooling

Cook: 2 hours 5 mins,
plus standing

Ingredients

85 g/3 oz unsalted butter, melted

140 g/5 oz digestive biscuits, crushed

300 g/10½ oz strawberries, hulled

600 g/1 lb 5 oz full fat soft cheese

225 g/8 oz caster sugar

2 large eggs, beaten

2 tbsp cornflour

finely grated rind and juice of 1 lemon

Method

1 Stir the butter into the crushed biscuits and press into the base of a 20-cm/8-inch round springform tin, or a tin that fits into your slow cooker.

2 Purée or mash half the strawberries and whisk together with the cheese, sugar, eggs, cornflour, lemon rind and juice until smooth.

3 Tip the mixture into the tin and place in the slow cooker. Cover and cook on high for about 2 hours or until almost set.

4 Turn off the slow cooker and leave the cheesecake in the cooker for 2 hours. Remove and cool completely, then carefully turn out of the tin.

5 Decorate with the remaining sliced strawberries and serve.

MINI PUMPKIN CHEESECAKES WITH GINGERNUT CRUST

Serves: 4

Prep: 20–25 mins, plus cooling & chilling

Cook: 2 hours 12 mins, plus standing

Ingredients

Base

115 g/4 oz gingernut biscuits, crushed

2 tbsp soft light brown sugar

pinch of salt

3 tbsp unsalted butter, melted

Topping

1 tbsp flour

¼ tsp ground cinnamon

pinch of grated nutmeg

pinch of salt

2 large eggs

100 g/3½ oz soft light brown sugar

115 g/4 oz cream cheese

200 g/7 oz pumpkin purée

2 tbsp double cream

2 tsp vanilla extract

1 tbsp whisky

icing sugar, for dusting

Method

1 To make the base, preheat the oven to 190°C/375°F/Gas Mark 5. Put the crushed gingernuts, sugar and salt into a food processor and pulse several times. Add the butter and pulse until well combined. Press the mixture into the bases and about three quarters of the way up the sides of four 225-ml/8-fl oz ramekins. Place the ramekins on a baking tray and bake in the preheated oven for 10 minutes. Leave to cool.

2 To make the topping, put the flour, cinnamon, nutmeg and salt into a large bowl and whisk together. Whisk in the eggs, sugar, cream cheese, pumpkin purée, cream, vanilla extract and whisky.

3 Spoon the topping into the ramekins and place the ramekins in the slow cooker. Carefully add boiling water to a depth of 4 cm/1½ inches. Cover and cook on high for about 2 hours, until the filling is set. Turn off the slow cooker and leave the ramekins inside for a further 1 hour, then remove them from the slow cooker and chill in the refrigerator for at least 2 hours. Dust with icing sugar before serving.

CHOCOLATE FONDUE

Serves: 4–6   **Prep: 15 mins**   **Cook: 45–60 mins**

Ingredients

butter, for greasing

225 ml/8 fl oz double cream

350 g/12 oz plain chocolate, chopped into small pieces

1 tsp vanilla extract

To serve

diced fruit (bananas, strawberries, apples, pears)

marshmallows

cookies or pieces of cake

Method

1 Grease the inside of the slow cooker with butter.

2 Put the cream and chocolate into the slow cooker and stir to combine. Cover and cook on low, stirring occasionally, for 45–60 minutes, until the chocolate is completely melted. Stir in the vanilla extract.

3 Leave the mixture in the slow cooker or transfer to a fondue pot with a burner and serve immediately, with platters of diced fruit, marshmallows and cookies for dipping.

★ Variation

You can use milk or white chocolate instead of dark, if you prefer a fondue that isn't so rich. Just ensure that you always buy good-quality chocolate, whatever your preference.

INDEX

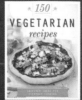

Introduction by Anne Sheasby
Cover photography by Ian Garlick
New internal photography by Sian Irvine

Notes for the Reader
This book uses both metric and imperial measurements. Follow the
same units of measurement throughout; do not mix metric and imperial.
All spoon measurements are level: teaspoons are assumed to be 5 ml,
and tablespoons are assumed to be 15 ml. Unless otherwise stated, milk
is assumed to be full fat, eggs and individual vegetables are medium,
and pepper is freshly ground black pepper. Unless otherwise stated, all
root vegetables should be peeled prior to using.

Garnishes, decorations and serving suggestions are all optional and
not necessarily included in the recipe ingredients or method. The
times given are an approximate guide only. Preparation times differ
according to the techniques used by different people and the cooking
times may also vary from those given. Optional ingredients, variations or
serving suggestions have not been included in the time calculations.

INDEX